igniting
the inner life

Other Books by Regina Sara Ryan

The Wellness Workbook: How to Achieve Enduring Health & Vitality, with John W. Travis, M.D.

Simply Well: Choices for a Healthy Life, with John W. Travis, M.D.

After Surgery, Illness or Trauma: 10 Steps to Renewed Energy and Health

No Child in My Life

Everywoman's Book of Common Wisdom, with Erica Jen and Lalitha Thomas

The Woman Awake: Feminine Wisdom for Spiritual Life

Praying Dangerously: Radical Reliance on God

Breastfeeding: Your Priceless Gift to Your Baby and Yourself, with Deborah Auletta, IBCLC

Only God: A Biography of Yogi Ramsuratkumar

igniting
the inner life

Regina Sara Ryan

HOHM PRESS
Prescott, Arizona

Cover Design: www.adizuccarello.com
Interior Design and Layout: www.kadakgraphics.com

PERMISSIONS and poetry credits are listed on pages 236–237.

Library of Congress Cataloging-in-Publication Data

Ryan, Regina Sara.
  Igniting the inner life / Regina Sara Ryan.
    p. cm.
  Includes bibliographical references (p.   ) and index.
  ISBN 978-1-935387-17-6 (trade pbk. : alk. paper)
  1. Spiritual life. I. Title.
  BL624.R875 2010
  204'.4--dc22

                                    2010022843

HOHM PRESS
P.O. Box 2501
Prescott, AZ 86302
800-381-2700
www.hohmpress.com

This book was printed in the U.S.A. on recycled, acid-free paper using soy ink.

"But all, yes all, in order to be true
must arise out of Love
be consumed in Love
and return to Love.
Thus asserts the true heart-son
of the Maddest Love of All,
Yogi Ramsuratkumar, the crazy Beggar …"

Lee Lozowick, 7 May 1998
Gasping For Air in a Vacuum, 208.

Contents

Introduction

Life for us has become an endless affair of trying to improve ourselves: achieving more and doing more, learning more, always needing to know more things. The process of learning and being taught has simply become a matter of being fed facts and information—receiving what we didn't have before, always being given something different from ourselves.

That's why whatever we learn never touches us deeply enough, why nothing really satisfies us. And the more we sense this the more we rush around trying to find other substitutes to fill the void we still feel inside. Everything pushes us outside ourselves—farther away from the utter simplicity of our own humanity.

— Peter Kingsley, *In the Dark Places of Wisdom*, 188.

I read these words by Peter Kingsley on an airplane en route to Bucharest, Romania in the winter, 2009. Friends there had invited me to visit. For many years they had tempted me with the promise of making a pilgrimage to some of the ancient monasteries in the mountains north of this metropolitan capital. They wanted to share this journey with me knowing my own history within convent life and my great interest in prayer, in sacred art and in dynamic spirituality.

Peter Kingsley's book, *In the Dark Places of Wisdom*, was the perfect companion for such a pilgrim as I was. His stories of the wisdom traditions of the ancient Greeks—chiefly about Pythagoras and Parmenides—were full of radical although familiar reminding factors, like the one quoted above. That the essential nature of our humanity, including our spirituality, is *never* found "out there" was perfect advice for one on a journey to an "out there" that would, to my surprise and delight, amaze me at every turn.

Reflections on that pilgrimage and other pilgrimages I've made will flavor the chapters that follow. But first, I want to set the context in this book as a pilgrimage from "out there" to "in here." I want to remind myself *and you* of what we *know* in our own dark places of wisdom, but so often fail to grasp, to appreciate, and therefore to live, simply because we are so busy accumulating more stuff—more mediocre experiences and entertainments, more material things that then demand our time and attention, and more relationships that feed us junk food. Sadly, even among those of us who claim to hunger for an enlivened inner life, however we understand that term, the itch of "spiritual materialism" (a term given to us by the late Chögyam Trungpa Rinpoche) persists like a rash that won't go away. More books, more seminars, more methods, more more.

As Kingsley reflects in his revelatory book, the Pythagorean school emphasized "fewer answers and more riddles … less and less on being given teachings and more and more on finding the inner resources to discover your own answers inside yourself." (189) Of course this isn't news for you or me. And yet, I wonder, when will I stop long enough to let the truth of this saturate my cells? Tomorrow? Next vacation? Next retreat? When and how am I going to allow myself to become so soaked in this reality that my choices demonstrate it? I need courage, strength and joy to make this pilgrimage "home." Maybe this book, despite its form in offering words from "out there," can actually be another reminder that the wisdom abides within.

In my previous book *Praying Dangerously*, I advised readers to put the book down and start praying. With this one, I urge you to remember that you don't *need* what I'm going to write about. On the other hand, I don't recommend that you throw the book away. Rather, you might use it the way I use dozens of daily reminding factors—to momentarily wake me up and to remind me of what I know.

Because It Is Your Delight

Writing this book has been my delight. Sharing it with anybody else is my delight. I hope that you read it in delight. This word "delight" has entered my vocabulary lately with gentle intensity, substituting regularly for a bunch of nouns that I formerly staked my reputation on. Nouns like "prayer" or "meditation" or "work" or "service." It has especially driven out a score of verbs like "struggle" or "help" or "search." Simply and blessedly, it has begun to characterize my relationship to my spiritual mentor, and to what was previously a burden of learning to improve myself, *trying* to help others, and trying to convince people that I was a good and trustworthy person so they would approve of me.

In the dictionary, the word "delight" used as a noun is defined as *great pleasure or joy*. As a verb, it means *to take* great pleasure or joy in something. This is a radical substitution for me—to be more often celebrating and expressing my delight in this pilgrimage that is my life, as opposed to soldiering my way through it. At sixty-five years of age it's probably about time! After all, many wise old women have instructed me that one of the benefits of aging is that you might give up caring what others think about you.

The root of the word *delight* is the Latin *delectare*, which means "to entice." How delightful. Children are enticed into a game because they see others having a wonderful time; they are enticed into forgetting their tears when their attention is re-directed to some task that causes them joy; they are enticed to take their much needed medicine by mother's soft and comforting words. Such enticements are not promises of pleasure and joy in the future as much as they are expressions of immediate pleasure and joy that are irresistible.

But, before I go much further, let me advise you that my delight is not about "doing my own thing" in the way that term is often applied, which sometimes means at the expense of other's sensitivities. It also has nothing to do with wearing purple shoes, or red hats, with my gray hair streaming in the breeze, or strolling around being a liberated granny and saying whatever's on my mind. Please don't box and wrap my expression of delight, pleasure or joy in a package labeled "magical coincidences"; or imagine that it includes only stories about warm puppies and Christmas mornings, or revelations from God given in a candlelit cathedral. That type of limitation would be a shame, I think. To limit the whole range of life experience in this way would disallow me the privilege of delighting in darkness, in confusion, in chaos, in the insecurity of not knowing what comes next. Perhaps, as I have, you've shared the "delight" of cleaning the vomit or the shit from a beloved friend's body as she or he was dying. There is real joy in assuring your beloved that this task is your privilege to accomplish for her; that she has no cause to be embarrassed in your presence; that the love you share has equalized the tasks you can perform for one another.

Noble and Dignified

For me, delight is a function of appreciating that my essential nature is characterized by "intrinsic nobility" and "intrinsic dignity." These delicious, highly tangible descriptions were integral to the teaching of a twentieth-century saint from western Bengal, India, named Swami Prajnanpad. And that same understanding is expressed by other saints and sages, contemporary or ancient. "Basic goodness" is the way that Chögyam Trungpa referred to it; and "organic innocence" and "wise innocence" are the words of my own spiritual teacher of twenty-six years, Lee Lozowick; and "the kingdom of heaven is within you" is how the master Jesus described it. When you get a glimpse of heaven, or dip your toes into genuine innocence, or bow down to the altar of basic goodness in yourself, well, delight often follows.

To rest in—or stand in—my own intrinsic dignity, inherent nobility or basic goodness brings with it the knowledge that everyone else *is* that too, at core. This engenders compassion (here I mean love penetrated by forgiveness) for myself and others: I know how often I forget the truth of my own nobility; I know how often you forget too. On this station platform of compassion, I am naturally motivated to talk to other men and women who are waiting for the same train that I am. Unfortunately, some are busy in the station gift shop; others are absorbed in their lattés in the station café, or fascinated by the clothes (or the biceps) of the other passengers, or wracking their brains for a good pick-up line. Consequently, they easily miss the station master's announcement and delay getting on the train.

But, for those who already have a foot on the step of the train car, luggage slung over their shoulders, a potential bond exists. We are on a journey, together, despite very different histories, and different descriptions of what we expect to find along the tracks ahead. Still, at this point in time, we each know something. We *know* that love *is*, or intrinsic nobility *is*, or however we express it. And we are determined to do what it takes to keep that knowledge fresh and in our faces. We know too that hanging out with others who share this knowledge and this intention is one of the best ways to keep it alive.

I invite you to read this book for your own delight. Read it because today we happen to have adjoining seats on the same train and because I'm telling stories about things that have delighted me recently. I'm telling, and you are listening, and hopefully becoming enticed into conversation with me. I'm telling stories because that is what I love to do, and what I'm good at. You are reading, I hope, because listening to stories delights you and reminds you of who you are, what you're doing here, and what you want. Perhaps my stories will entice you to tell your own delightful stories to another passenger or two on this train.

Who Wants This Book?

Igniting the Inner Life is a series of essays offered to those who are serious about their relationship to God, to prayer, to spiritual life, to Truth or Reality, whatever you call it, and also to those who, while believing that they don't really know for sure what this great inner mystery is, still feel irresistibly drawn to the subject of spiritual practice.

Perhaps you are one of this latter group. Perhaps you find certain music or ritual to be extremely powerful in connecting you to a domain of the heart's dominance, or to a sense of expansion of the usual definitions of self. Perhaps you are drawn to silence or solitude, knowing that something happens in these environments, although you're not exactly sure *what*.

Perhaps you intuit, despite all evidence, that you are connected to the whole in some numinous way. You intuit, and hope, that this connection means that your actions and intentions and prayers are making a difference on a larger scale. In any case, I hope these essays will prove useful to you. They come from my delight in being a friend to those who, while they have the desire and the willingness to practice, may lack the guidance to take that next risk, or that next step, to move into the darkness within. We all need guides and mentors, and today more than ever. Any heightened sense of urgency you feel in wanting to explore the inner life *now* is not an isolated phenomenon. The Earth is deeply imbalanced and human suffering and fear have surfaced in ways we never expected prior to September 11, 2001 in the U.S. and around the globe. Our terrors are guiding us and compelling us—the terrors of the collective psyche are building, and those with the sensitivity to feel such terrors are beginning to realize that they are carrying more than their own weight. This book is for those who seriously want to (or at least *want to* want to) assist humanity, and indeed all of creation, to find its way home.

Something Useful

Once a year for over twenty years my spiritual teacher Lee Lozowick would visit his own master Yogi Ramsuratkumar, the beggar saint of Tiruvannamalai, South India. Twice a day, large crowds would gather for the elder's darshan, to chant the name of God and to enjoy the mood of love that permeated the saint's presence. Whenever Lee was present, the old master would call him to the dais, bless him and ask him to "Say something useful to these people." Immediately Lee would bow, turn to the assemblage, and announce the directive: "Yogi Ramsuratkumar has asked me ..." He would then launch into telling stories about his teacher, whom he affectionately referred to as "my Father," or offering humble commentaries on his master's words, or inviting his listeners to live the practice of chanting the name of God. Whatever subject his speaking addressed, it was all simply a way of recounting the innumerable blessings that he had been given at his master's hand—blessings that were available to everyone.

As I begin this project I remember this directive given to Lee and take it as my own. "Something useful" is probably not so much about instruction, really. Something useful, as I've learned from my master, is first and foremost the praise of God; along with perhaps some stories that inspire, some brief commentaries on the words of the wise. There is no way of knowing if something is useful or not, as it depends upon the listener's, or in this case the reader's, response. Nonetheless, I'll give it my best shot, because it is simply delightful to sing such songs.

The essays that follow are all based in my explorations of the inner life. Some of them will be sweet and hopefully inspiring. Some of them, also hopefully, will be "kick-ass" and confronting, as these are among the many moods that delight me and keep me active in the realm of what really counts, for me! I will not "go gentle into that good night," as Dylan Thomas wrote to encourage his father's approach to death. I will be writing to break out of the illusory box that I've climbed into and that others want to keep me in.

There is no box, really. There is only a vast love. I pray to delight in all of it! Even when I can't *feel* loving or delight-full, I can *choose* delight, because feeling *what is* and remembering myself, as opposed to living in some fantasy of what should be or some overlay of distraction from the present moment, is joy; is true delight.

The inner journey ends where we can never map. The "Way" ultimately gets lost in the mist that surrounds the mountain's summit. As the author of the great classic *The Cloud of Unknowing* describes, we must: "Strike that thick cloud of unknowing with the sharp dart of longing love, and on no account whatever think of giving up."[1] Lighting, aiming and firing that dart, and doing it again and again and again, is what the inner life is about. Reminding you to avoid common missteps and helping you to plan and rely on rest stops within this magnificent quest is my small gift to you.

Ultimately, your intention will carry you through, despite dozens or even hundreds of delays and detours. This book is for those who want challenge, inspiration, motivation, companionship for the trip. Whatever is valuable here is simply that wisdom awakened in me by my guru and the great teachings of the ages. These teachings are with you too. Let us remember them together. And, let us never stray from telling the truth of what we know.

How Long Have We Forgotten How to Listen!

"Before they spring forth I tell you of them."—Isaiah, 42:9

How long have we forgotten how to listen?
He planted us once to listen
Planted us like lyme grass by the eternal sea,
We wanted to grow on fat pastures,
To stand like lettuce in the kitchen garden.
Although we have business
That lead us far
From his light,
Although we drink tap water,
And only as it dies it reaches
Our eternally thirsting mouths–
Although we walk down a street
Beneath which earth has been silenced
By a pavement,
We must not sell our ears,
Oh, we must not sell our ears.
Even in the market,
In the computation of dust,
Many had made a quick leap
Onto the tightrope of longing.
Because they heard something,
And leapt out of the dust
And sated their ears.
Press, oh press in the day of destruction
The listening ear to the earth,
And you will hear, through your sleep
You will hear,
How in death
Life begins.

—Nelly Sachs (1891-1970)[1]

Chapter 1

Love in the Time of Terror

When the World Trade Center fell on 9-11-2001, I was walking a quiet path to my teacher's ashram for morning meditation practice. After silent sitting for fifty minutes, followed by our usual chanting in honor of the guru, I ambled down to the ashram office to empty waste baskets and vacuum the rugs. My friend Sally met me at the entrance, her eyes wet, to tell me the news she had heard on the morning NPR broadcast. Her brother, who worked in Connecticut, had numerous clients in those buildings and, like so many others, Sally's first thoughts went to him and the safety of his family.

Unlike most of the inhabitants of the United States, we at the ashram didn't watch television or use the Internet in 2001. (We still don't watch TV.) I didn't see the horrifying image of the towers crumbling until years after the events took place. Nonetheless, I felt in my body the breathlessness of fear, grief and anxiety. My sister lives in Brooklyn and works four blocks from the World Trade Center. I tried unsuccessfully to call her.

With interest I noted that each of my friends—fellow students of my teacher—reverted to his or her familiar mode of dealing with grief. Some cried and partnered with someone else to talk to; I took control and looked around for how to keep business as usual going on in the office. It was a provocative lesson in self observation, if one had

1

the freedom to take it, as in: "This is what *I do* 'when the shit hits the fan,'" regardless of my protests of enlightened non-duality. Each of us felt the shock wave that rippled through the collective, and reacted however we were used to reacting to try to keep it together.

For me, the most impressive witness to the presence of a dynamic inner life in my sangha family was what happened during lunch that day. Gathered in the ashram living room, awaiting the opening prayer before eating, the children played with tinker toys and stuffed animals, and sang the songs they had sung every day for weeks. No one among the adults said a word about the panic and confusion that we each felt, more or less, and knew each other to be feeling. We prayed our meal prayer and carried on a conversation about the activities of our community blues band that was currently winding up their tour of Europe (we didn't know then that their return would be delayed by a week because of the event). We talked about what we always talk about, if we talk at all—books, movies, the progress of the garden, the guru's latest communication. And we enjoyed the children as we always do.

To their enormous credit, my brothers and sisters in the sangha held their individual and collective pain and allowed it to burn within, as they both protected our children—whom we all knew did not need to be infected with panic—and snapped up a chance to use a major moment of crisis for the transformational possibility it offered.

While I have no way of proving it, I'd bet that we were a thin minority in the country on that day, responding as we did. Over the weeks that followed, while we mourned with hearts open and shared stories of relatives and friends who were *there* or close by, and those who made it out alive, many of us deliberately chose not to immerse ourselves in the media coverage of the event even when we had the chance. In so doing we were making a radical choice, for which some will label us naïve or even uncaring. But, as I appreciated then and still do, this choice was a clear vote in favor of the inner life and a commitment toward awakening from the dream of separation, over and against an identification with the "sleeping world" view, which sees and languages everything in terms of panic and scarcity; a stand contrary to the cultural matrix in which love is not Ground Zero, despite the tales of heroic self-sacrifice that canonized genuine saints on the spot that day and for months afterward.

As an interesting aside, I've frequently asked myself whether I missed anything by not hearing the speeches of Rudy Giuliani or watching the replay of the tragedy ad infinitum, or learning who did what when or who knew what when? Consider this for yourself. Are you really different as a result of this Earth-shaking interference? I know that New Yorkers were different, for a while. My sister and brother live there and they each had dozens of very personal stories to tell, and what they lacked personally *The New York Times* supplied every day for months—page after page of photos and stories.

But, I ask myself again, are any of us really transformed? Are any of us more aware of our own mechanical, crystallized habits—the habits that keep us hitting our heads against the same wall of the same maze, day and night?

Welcome to our world! Your desire for an intensified inner life will not keep you in bliss, obviously. If it is genuine, it will take you into the midst of this world. For some, that will mean Baghdad or Kabul, or the AIDS ward at a major hospital, or the inner city classroom. For others, it will demand a retreat to the desert for a significant period of prayer and even fasting; or it may involve a decision to move back "home" to take care of aging parents. Whatever form you are destined to pursue (and I don't use this word "destined" lightly, as I'm a firm believer that the ego, with which we generally identify, is *not* running the show), you will be challenged to live that form either from the outside in or the inside out. Falling into fear, or buying into the culture's norms about *anything*, will be a major detour in your journey along this highway of consciousness and compassionate life.

In these terrorizing times we need to clearly see the characteristics of the *kali yuga* around us and *choose* to be here, rather than merely resigning ourselves to resisting or reacting against its evils. (The *kali yuga* is one of four great ages or stages that the world cycles through, as set forth in the Sanskrit scriptures. The "kali" of *kali yuga* should not be understood as referring to the Goddess Kali, but rather to a time of strife, discord, quarrel, or contention.) Even when the forces of darkness are apparently winning, we will always have a choice.

Elder Justin's Message

The highpoint of my trip to Romania in the spring of 2009 was a visit to a monastery in Petru Voda, in the Carpathian Mountains about six hours north of Bucharest. I was brought there by friends who knew of a living saint, known familiarly as Father Justin Parvu, a ninety-one-year-old monk, who had been imprisoned by the Communists for nearly twenty years during the 1970s and 80s. After the Romanian Revolution of 1989, the priest wanted nothing better than to move into permanent hermitage to pursue his contemplative life, but young religious men in the newly liberated church begged him to guide them. The result was that in 1991 a monastery was built near the tiny village, accessible only by a muddy dirt road, and this saintly man (in his 70s) took up residence there. For twenty years since then he has continued to guide the younger monks, and to serve as a wise elder for Romanian Orthodox Christians throughout the country.

On the rainy March day of my visit, our traveling party of three was told that that we were lucky to have come on an off-day. We would have a short wait, perhaps only four or five hours, to receive our audience with the old man, who sits in a tiny cluttered room from early morning until late at night, greeting and blessing the hundreds of people who come to him. Most come with requests for prayers—a dying husband, a sick child, a change of job. Others seek his intervention in their immediate difficulties—helping them to work out marital difficulties, or seeking his advice for dealing with rebellious children. One and all, he greets them, blesses them, and with no hurry or need to keep a schedule (if you don't get in today, well there's always to-morrow), he listens to their stories, their pain, and offers his simple but effective counsel.

A printed notice at the entrance to Father Justin's room invites his visitors to listen carefully to the exact words he will use in speaking to them. It warns them to not dismiss any details during their time with him. Father Justin will be performing a type of surgery on your soul, it says, and you may feel the effects in a variety of ways in your life, so be aware.

I had no petition for the elder, but I did wish his bless-ing. Having spent five weeks in the physical presence of my teacher's guru Yogi Ramsuratkumar in 1995, I could testify to the life-transforming energy that such a holy one transmits. I was not going to miss the opportunity for a blessing from a Romanian sage. Whether this man proved a charlatan or not, I figured it was worth the wait to find out.

Father Justin greeted us with smiling eyes and no fanfare, despite the fact that a visit from an American was exceptionally rare (as I was later told). He seemed genuinely delighted when we told him that we had no questions or requests but wanted only his blessing. "You have come all this way to see an old Romanian man who does nothing," he said with genuine candor. Father Justin obliged our request generously, anointing our hands (on the tops and on the palms) and our foreheads with holy oil. He gifted us with crosses blessed in Jerusalem, and with small prayer cards (in Romanian of course) depicting St. George killing a dragon. And he joked with us about the tendencies of Americans versus the tendencies of Romanians: ask an American a question and you're liable to hear his excuse that he has to come back three days later with his answer. Ask a Romanian a question and he's answered you before the words are fully out of your mouth.

I didn't feel like I'd endured psychic or spiritual surgery when I left him. But, truth be told, I've told the story of meeting him to dozens of people, individually or in groups, since that wondrous day. Fr. Justin "got in," and everyone who hears about him seems touched by whatever small detail I relate.

Because we are considering the subject of fear, the cultural mindset, and its relationship to the life of the spirit, Fr. Justin has a poignant witness to bear. His monastic life, far from being the quiet contemplative retreat that he envisioned as a young man, was regularly interspersed with periods of persecution—imprisonment and torture—and now is fully dedicated to the needs of others. If Fr. Justin wants his quiet time for contemplation, he finds it at night, as I was told that he sits in the monastery church from 11 PM until 3 AM, when the rest of the monks gather for prayer.

I imagine that the old monk is no stranger to fear, and because the fear of death apparently has no more power over him, he can serve now as a prophetic voice crying out in this wilderness of the technological age. Begging his Romanian people to remember their history and their ultimate roots in the lineage of a crucified Christ, he urges them to return to their soul's center.

For several years now, so many people, full of fear, have been coming to him with questions about the current and the coming times that he has written a letter addressing the issue. Everyone who visits him now is given a copy of it. In brief, the letter announces that he reads the signs around him and is convinced that we are in the end times. For him, the "end times" equate to the fact that the forces of the world, the flesh, the devil … and technology! (lots of descriptive words apply) have triumphed in our day. As much as he would like to encourage us that there is still hope to turn around the enormous tide of godless materialism and greed and violence, he believes that it is simply too late.

Father Justin's message is not a happy one. And, he is certainly not alone in his view of the current state of affairs. From biologists, conservationists, politicians, shaman of the rare indigenous tribes that are still attuned to some primal Earth-based knowledge, and a wide variety of spiritual teachers, the message is similar. According to the paradigm of the cycle of ages in Hinduism, we are deeply mired in the kali yuga right now—the age of deterioration and destruction.

His message is more than an expression of helplessness and hopelessness, however. If Father Justin had given me nothing but this dire warning I would have left him feeling depressed too; not at all impassioned to share his story. But, quite the contrary, his joyful presence seemed to emanate light; he inspired me and filled me with hope. Father Justin's being was obviously large enough to contain extremes, and even contradictions. While serving as a prophet of the end times, he was also a prophet of the metanoia—"a new mind." His suffering has taught him well that in times of persecution and deprivation the human spirit is given opportunities to return to its innate wisdom, its core values. Father Justin calls his people to remember the early days following Christ's crucifixion, recalling that the blood of martyrs had nourished God's kingdom on earth. Radical times, he reminds them, call for radical measures. It is time to return to the land of your soul, he says in his own way, and take stock of what you find there.

One of the most poignant messages that Father Justin shared was a call to memorize the scriptures. He said that this injunction was a frequent request from early Church elders, and bore re-examination today. The holy books or scriptures of any religious or spiritual tradition are among the first items either co-opted or destroyed when one culture overtakes another. If, however, these teachings are encoded in the body-mind, they are forever accessible, no matter what happens in the external forum.

My teacher Lee Lozowick expanded upon this bit of instruction by saying that once the scriptures are all digitalized, humans will collectively breathe a sigh of relief, imagining naively that somehow these wisdom teachings are now safe. But, he cautions, this naïve assumption will only cloud us with a false sense of security that will discourage our passion for learning the scriptures with the heart. In simple terms, we all suffer this naiveté when we buy a book and then forget about it. How may unopened books are gathering dust on your shelves? And yet, at the time they were purchased or collected, they probably brought some sense of satisfaction: "*If* I ever need to find out anything about this subject, I'll know right where to look." But to catalog the contents of a book does not mean that one has absorbed or integrated its message.

When I returned to the States after this momentous trip, I stayed my first night with my friend Elizabeth whom I knew would appreciate the nature of my pilgrimage. As we shared a simple supper, we were joined by another friend, Maureen, who listened to the stories with similar enthusiasm. When I got to the part about the "end times," I held back a bit in my descriptions. After all, I was a guest, and really didn't want to discomfort my hosts too much, right away. But Maureen wouldn't let me off the hook. She wanted to know it all. The more I spoke, the more her eyes widened, and the more radiant her face became. And then she said something that turned everything over; something that I will never forget, as long as I live. "Oh my, how blessed we are," Maureen said. "I feel so honored that our Lord has called me to serve his work in the end times, when other people are going to need help the most!"

Maureen is obviously a committed Christian. She languages her dedication in the words of her own faith tradition—that of serving her Lord Jesus. Yet her comment has universal application to anyone who seeks a genuine inner life, a path of the heart. We could just as easily say that Maureen's remark revealed the soul of a *bodhisattva*. This

Buddhist term describes one who willingly returns to the fray, lifetime after lifetime, with the sole intention of helping all other sentient beings to realize their true nature. Regardless of circumstances, and often most in the worst of times, the inner life can flourish. When we are ready to re-contextualize our lives from a fear-based struggle for survival to a love-infused offer of service, we can say so. I believe that a genuine cry to heaven, one that voices our intention for a life beyond fear and a life dedicated to real service—a life lived from the inside out—will be heard.

~

I placed this chapter at the opening of the book deliberately. Simply, I wanted to re-ignite my own sense of urgency for inner work—prayer, practice, self-remembrance—because I know that these are the roots from which genuine compassion and right service grow and flower. Rushing around doing good, building false security that we are getting somewhere, is a bit like rearranging the deck chairs on the Titanic. Simply spinning our praying wheels or hoping for salvation, expecting the hand of God to pull us out of the mess, can be another waste of precious time. Terrible times call for serious measures, and one way or another, humans have always faced terrible times. Those who "Know Thyself"—in the most universal sense—have a better chance at exercising the clarity, discrimination, non-attachment, and courageous efforts necessary in the face of terror.

I am proposing that we reconceive the dream. That we consider what would happen if security were not the point of existence. That we find freedom, aliveness and power not from what contains,

locates, or protects us, but from what dissolves, reveals and expands us. —Eve Ensler [2]

As we consider in the chapters ahead what the inner
life may include, what discourages it and what builds it, I
urge you to keep your eyes and your heart and your ears
open to the suffering world in which you live. Our job,
aboard a ship that is going down, is to remember for ourselves and to remind our fellow passengers how to live
underwater.

Last night, as I was sleeping,
I dreamt—marvelous error!—
that a spring was breaking
out in my heart.
I said: Along which secret aqueduct,
oh water, are you coming to me,
water of a new life
that I have never drunk?

Last night, as I was sleeping,
I dreamt—marvelous error!—
that I had a beehive
here inside my heart.
And the golden bees
were making white combs
and sweet honey
from my old failures.

Last night, as I was sleeping,
I dreamt—marvelous error!—
that a fiery sun was giving
light inside my heart.
It was fiery because I felt
warmth as from a hearth,
and sun because it gave light
and brought tears to my eyes.

Last night, as I slept,
I dreamt—marvelous error!—
that it was God I had
here inside my heart.

—Antonio Machado[1]

Chapter 2

The Inner Life

Everyone has an inner life. In the most general sense, the inner life consists of whatever we attend to "inside": our thoughts, feelings, plans, hopes, tensions and bodily sensations.

Usually, the immediate content and experience of this inner life is kept somewhat to oneself. Society frowns upon individuals who seem to have no boundaries here—people who complain constantly, or who walk around narrating aloud the blips of their inner awareness. The better-adapted among us have learned to keep our thoughts and feelings under wraps, sharing them at what we judge to be the right moment, like when we have a decent listener, or when it's actually time to make the plan, or when we can't endure one more moment of frustration. Of course, even when we aren't describing our inner life out loud, in words, we betray ourselves, as our posture, our facial expressions, the tone of our voice and the tension in our shoulders give us away. Nevertheless, most of us have an unspoken agreement, a contract with those around us, that we'll pretend their external signs of contradiction don't exist, as we continue to interact with one another based on the surface of things.

We don't know ourselves.

All Kinds of Inner Life

I asked the women in a workshop I conducted to discuss

the question: "What do you mean by the inner life?" They each had a slightly different (some had a radically different) take on the subject. The question is worth asking: "What do *I* mean by the inner life? And, what ignites it?"

One woman glared at the rest of us saying, "I never speak about my inner life with anybody else." Others talked about the necessity of listening to that creative voice—the muse—who inspires their art; or listening to their heart, which will indicate a direction. A few described moments of bliss, transcendence, an experience of being outside themselves and finding they were not separate from love. Another young woman noted that she studies her dreams; an elder remarked that for her it was about prayer and being in the presence of God.

As different as these expressions were, a few common threads emerged in all of them. Almost all agreed that the inner life was marked by some deviation from the status quo—from the life of the herd. An inner life was synonymous, therefore, with a certain freedom. Almost all agreed that the inner life was generally discovered and nurtured by taking time alone. And, this notion of the heart and its knowledge was integral to almost everybody's description. Finally, they all used the term "journey" or "path" or "way" as they described their own processes.

The Inner Life / The Inner Journey

To ignite the inner *life* is not essentially different from making the inner journey that is presented in every authentic religious, spiritual and philosophical tradition. While the signposts along the way may be written in a variety of languages, and rest stops painted in different colors, the route they mark generally goes to the same place—or *no place*, as the case may be! Igniting the inner life is the metaphor I use for the process we all endure and participate in once we discover that there is more to life than meets the eye.

A vague inclination to go "somewhere else" is enough to get one started on this journey. But a clear and articulated intention alerts and invites help from unexpected quarters. It is valuable, therefore, to make some distinctions about this process, to refine our understanding of ourselves, and to sharpen our discriminating faculties about what's *out there* and what's *in here*. Detours, distractions and dead-ends abound. As you know, without discrimination you can easily pull out the immature radishes in your garden leaving behind only the uninvited prairie grass. And while there is nothing wrong with prairie grass, it is simply not useful for your salad, and may in fact be seriously damaging to your purpose—in this case, by choking your radishes.

When we are able to pinpoint and thus describe the differences in things—in various qualities, in people, in methodologies—we have a powerful tool to advance our intention. One aim of this book is to encourage you, and even to guide you at times, in specifying and thus enhancing your purpose with regard to the inner life.

"What do you want?" is the question that the wise elder in any tradition asks the naïve aspirant every time. "What have you come here for?" "What is it you seek?" "Whom do you seek?" "Where do you want to go?" "What can I do for you?" And the response given is often *the* determining factor in whether the seeker will be admitted to the master's immediate company on the mountain, or sent down to the valley's elementary school for a few years.

So, let me ask you that question, here in these opening pages of our encounter. "What do you want?" "What are you expecting as you examine the inner life?" "What do you need?" It is difficult to know what route to choose if you don't know what you're heading for, and for that reason I will continue to urge you to articulate and thus refine your purpose. And, sometimes the destination you articulate won't really matter; sometimes a road trip to anywhere simply has its own rewards. The path itself *is* the goal, says the Tibetan Buddhist teacher Chögyam Trungpa Rinpoche, and I'll keep reminding you of this distinction as we pilgrimage together.

Distinctions change everything. Like when you give a friend the word "grief" to designate her current state of confusion, depression, anger, and emotional paralysis followed by hair-trigger volatility. My friend Rita had been using the term "going crazy" to relate to her surprising upsets. When I suggested that her mother's death six months ago, coupled with her recent loss of a job, were events that needed to be mourned and integrated rather than endured bravely, she was visibly relieved. The great researcher in death and dying, Dr. Elisabeth Kübler-Ross, gave us all that distinction when she explained the nature of grief-work. I was merely reminding Rita.

Or how about the distinction I learned from a hermit monk who lives in the desert of southern Arizona. A woman thanked him for his service and sacrifice, saying that she so appreciated the work that monks were doing on behalf of all. "I'm not doing it for you," he said. "Everybody has to do his or her own work," he told her, in terms that cut through her sentimentality. He explained that the monk does his or her *own* work and often, amazingly, that just happens to benefit others by reminding them that they have to do theirs. The monk's job is to *remember* himself or herself in God. If that models what the rest of us have to do, and we are inspired, so much the better!

My function in this book will be to make some distinctions, to the best of my ability. When the road gets rough, these distinctions will perhaps serve to warn you in advance; sometimes they will indicate a useful detour. You may consider me your witness and companion on this journey.

Some explorations of the inner life are circuitous, they tend to frustrate the seeker until he or she finally gives up logical control. Some journeys are apparently dangerous; they leave you raw and vulnerable and fearing that you are going mad. Others look easy and smooth at first, like this simple recommendation to "live by the heart." These pilgrimages are often ecstatic, light-filled at the superficial levels. As the soul proceeds along this way, however, it finds the discarded backpacks and plastic water bottles left by previous companions. The once-lovely pilgrimage then becomes a test of endurance, demanding long and unexpected encounters with loneliness, fear and emptiness. Author Edwin Bernbaum in *The Way to Shambhala: A Search for the Mythical Kingdom Beyond the Himalayas* offered seekers this wise counsel more than thirty years ago:

> Much of the inner journey consists of bringing the contents of the subconscious—especially the repressed and alienated parts of the surface consciousness—to awareness in order to face and master them. This happens when we begin to awaken elements from the deeper levels of mind. Since repressed material from the surface consciousness has attached itself to these elements, it comes up too, giving us the characteristic experience of discovering something that seems bad for everything good that we uncover in ourselves. Many of the

horrifying demons of the journey, for example, embody the horror we feel at finding hidden failings in ourselves that we despise others for having. Not only does this threaten the integrity of our egos, but even worse, it threatens to release an agonizing flood of self-loathing. As a result, we see these alienated parts of the surface consciousness—and the awareness of their existence—as dangerous and terrifying monsters that we must avoid. They become obstacles that we dare not face, much less attempt to overcome. Yet only by doing so can we dispel our illusory images of ourselves and proceed along the path to liberation. In facing our inner obstacles, and the pain and dismay they entail, we purify our minds and clarify our perceptions of reality. (208)

And so, as we engage *Igniting the Inner Life*, we need our eyes open, a deep sense of humility, and a heavy dose of patience and persistence. Compassion too, of course. As Bernbaum notes, we tend to fuel the fires of self-loathing as we encounter the lies, the deceptions, the ignorance and naiveté we have been living with and calling "real life" for so long. I can't go to the heart of this mandala (which is also the heart of a vast labyrinth) without facing these monsters. Only a warrior of the inner life makes this journey. To sit in silence, allowing Truth to emerge from its cave, will be terrifying at times. And while that Truth certainly includes the habits of our lies and deceptions, what is sometimes more terrifying to face is the heat of love that pours forth from these depths. As we undertake this investigation together, we'll encounter some of this fear and loathing, and hopefully some of this great underpinning of love. So take courage.

Based in my own self-explorations, this book is loosely structured to cover a variety of distinctions about of the inner life and how to ignite it, including:

- the practice of **self observation**, leading to a clearer view of what we're up to (radical self honesty), and to a sense of "being presence"—the awareness of ourselves alive and breathing, *as we are*, of life's flow within and around us, and where this leads
- the practice of **prayer**, or the offering of merit—building the alignment with God or Source through devotion and remembrance, through breath, through service
- and the cultivation of the creative **art of the heart**—through resting in our intrinsic dignity and nobility (Swami Prajnanpad), through love, deep listening and feeding one's truest art.

Others have looked at the inner life differently—with a focus on dreams or symbolism, for example—and their work has served me tremendously. I make no claims to presenting an exhaustive overview here. This book will simply visit a number of chambers of the interior castle and encourage me to stoke the fires in these hearths. But first, it will be important to draw another distinction that will set a context for everything else, a vital distinction that anyone who explores the inner dimension (especially if he or she calls it "spiritual" life) needs to hold clearly.

A Body of Wisdom

Who I Am inhabits a physical body. The body is real! It pains me, sometimes so powerfully that I am thrown to my knees to claw at the dirt and cry out for relief. It pleasures me too, as my senses are overwhelmed by sex, by a taste, by music or the sound of a child's voice, by the aroma of mother's soup or the incense in the temple, by the view of an uninterrupted expanse of sea or sky, by warmth when I come in from the cold, by the wonder of light, in day or night. As such, it is my greatest reminding factor.

There is no escaping the reality of this body, although God knows I try! Moment after moment this body delivers a Fed-Ex'd letter of reality to my doorstep, notifying me of the abiding truth of this moment, and of impermanence. "Nothing lasts," it declares. "You too will be a corpse," announces Chögyam Trungpa Rinpoche.

The body is both a microcosm of the universe and a macrocosm of its individual cells. It teaches the profound truth of interdependence—a spiritual principal found in every great religious tradition. We are not discrete entities floating in some vast cosmic puddle. We humans are connected to all and everything, within and without, toxified or invigorated because the air we breathe is poisonous or pure. We are not separate from the life force that created us and the life force that sustains us. Every system within our physical body relies on every other system. My feet, my lungs, my skeletal system, my bowels—these are not transcendable. Nor are they somehow lesser than my heart, brain, eyes; nor simply baggage to haul around while the serious business of spirituality or service gets done. Any rhetoric about the inner life that separates it from the life of the whole body, or that urges us to transcend the reality of embodiment, is a lie.

The body is my ticket to the natural world, a vast training ground for what it means to live true to my nature. I am made of the same stuff as the rabbits and the stars. I look at great trees and I am stabilized in my roots. I immerse myself in water and I am renewed. When I care for something or someone I often express it with my limbs or my face in contact with them—I hug my grandchild, I kiss my husband, I ruffle the dog's fur, I hold the hand of my dying father. In and with *this body* I love the Earth.

Please be aware that I'm writing this section for myself. As a great writing coach once instructed, you write in order to find out what you know. Here I'm attempting to make distinctions *for myself* about the mystery and reality of the body and the nature of the inner life. It is a subject of ongoing wonder and a challenge for me, as I'm so often swept away by the desire to find some place beyond all *this*, someplace where chaos, dirty dishes, insecurity and suffering can't touch. So, be forewarned, I'm often in the dark here, which is probably a good thing. I'm on the path *with* you.

You should have a sense of self-respect and self-comfort throughout your life. When you walk down the street, don't rush. Just take a nice walk. Be yourself, appreciate yourself. Even appreciate your subconscious thoughts. Appreciate that you are a human being in one piece. Your arms and your legs and your head are not flying off everywhere because of your wild thoughts, but you remain as one good human being with your shoes and your hairdo, perhaps wearing glasses, a tie and jacket, walking on the good earth, on the good street. Just do that, just walk nicely. Just do it. Then you will begin to feel that you are doing your real job. It's not even a job, but you are actually being what you should be. After that, you can learn to eat properly, drink properly, even pee properly.
—Chögyam Trungpa [2]

In Christ's Body

I *know* that St. Symeon's directive in the poem that follows is true. *How* I know this is because it causes holy aspiration to arise in me. It taps something essential and draws me out of my self-obsession with guilt, fear, pain. For a moment, at least, it wakes me up.

> We awaken in Christ's body
> as Christ awakens our bodies,
> and my poor hand is Christ, He enters
> my foot, and is infinitely me.
>
> I move my hand, and wonderfully
> my hand becomes Christ, becomes all of Him
> (for God is indivisibly
> whole, seamless in His Godhood).
>
> I move my foot, and at once
> he appears like a flash of lightning.
> Do my words seem blasphemous?—Then
> open your heart to Him
>
> and let yourself receive the one
> who is opening to you so deeply.
> For if we genuinely love Him,
> we wake up inside Christ's body
> where all our body, all over,
> every most hidden part of it,
> is realized in joy as Him,
> and He makes us, utterly real,
>
> and everything that is hurt, everything

that seemed to us dark, harsh, shameful,
maimed, ugly, irreparably
damaged, is in Him transformed

and recognized as whole, as lovely,
and radiant in His light.
We awaken as the Beloved
in every last part of our body.
　　　　—St. Symeon the New Theologian (949-1022)[3]

Symeon's words speak of the interplay of macrocosm and microcosm and give a new spin to the subject under consideration. This inner life that we consider here is not merely about what's inner *to me*, but about what I am *inner to*. In other words, as the contemporary mystic Bernadette Roberts said, it is not so much about "God in me" as it is about "me in God." And as Kahlil Gibran wrote decades ago: "When you love you should not say, 'God is in my heart,' but rather, 'I am in the heart of God.'"[4]

The "me in God" perspective ... whether God is named the Beloved, the guru, the great cosmic dance, Love, the Tao, Jesus, Divine Mother ... changes everything. It necessitates a view of non-separation, as it includes all of me—body, mind, emotions—not just my so-called spiritual parts, while including all of you—the challenged and suffering and ecstatic world of all sentient beings. It hits me with the reality that I cannot pray alone except as I pray in and with and as all of us. At the same time, for all its cosmic overtones, this perspective enlivens and focuses my attention within my own chest. I am more in touch than ever with the sacred potential of this body of mine, in this moment, and with the secret of love that enflames *me* with longing, and arouses my prayers on behalf of everything.

An Image of the Inner Life

The pregnant Mother Mary carrying the Christ child in *her* body is an image I like to contemplate. Now, before some of you reject this picture because it reminds you of your old fifth-grade catechism class, or because so many images of Mother Mary are just too saccharine to swallow, give me a break. Besides, isn't this only the mind projecting the past onto the present, and thus limiting what might be a very useful experience?

Honestly, I could just as well conjure for you an image of my friend Claire, seven months pregnant and stroking her belly, speaking soft words of encouragement and reassurance to the child in her womb and glowing with the wonder of their secret relationship—a secret that everybody around her assumes they know. Fact is, the rest of us see only the external signs of this bond, this love affair. As beautiful as it appears, their inner life is a sacred treasure, a secret, and Claire is only sharing a tiny fragment of it with us. She can't do otherwise, even though she is a poet. At best, she can hint at such love in words, but mostly she can simply shine the radiance of her face in our direction and heave a deep sigh.

I offer this image because the question on the table is how to live in the awareness of "God in me" *and* "me in God" as we turn our attention to the inner life. And my answer for myself in this moment is that remembering the Madonna and child—Maria, or Claire—is one of those ways. Whether we are male or female, whether we have ever borne a child in our body or not, the pregnant woman, radiant with life force, is an archetype that we can probably *feel* into. Without too much trouble I can imagine what it would be like to carry a secret, a wonder that cannot be easily expressed, but neither can it be forgotten because it is so damn real. Every time I tried to squeeze into a seat on a bus, there it would be. Every time I bent over to tie my Reeboks, there it would be. Every time I overate, or passed by a mirror, or turned over in bed, or saw another pregnant woman on the street, there it would be. And it would kick, this little secret of mine. It would move, it would give me constant feedback. And, if I were like Claire, I would constantly pay attention and constantly be in prayer, awestruck at the miracle of my body, humbled by the sacred responsibility entrusted to me. I would "get" that I was part of a greater mystery, or as my friend Claire told me, "That something larger than me had taken me up." I was a vehicle designed for the preservation of the species, true, and over and above all that I was a mother in love with her unborn child.

No wonder Mother Mary sang the "Magnificat" when she encountered her cousin Elizabeth, who was also pregnant. Who else could relate to such humility and hubris in one: "Magnificat" ... what magnificence! "Anima mea Dominum" ... my soul exalts in the Lord, the Mighty, who has done great things to me ... and from now on all generations will call me blessed. Both "in God" and "God in" perspectives are contained in this.

When I am overlooking the sacred in everything, I can see pregnancy as merely the commonplace process that it is. Remembering, I can view it with eyes widened within the archetype. The precious life that stirs in *me now*, that is not separate from *us now*, is the essence of God's own life, God's love. And that recognition would carry an overwhelming sense of both humility and responsibility, as I know it does for Claire.

A Sufi master once instructed his disciples in this reality using the words, "Your body is the Blessed Virgin Mary." He went on to remind his listeners, "You each carry the Christ child within you, and will birth that child, and will be asked to feed and protect that child." And in this teaching we have a ripe reminder of the inner life, and a call to a degree of attention that can serve us forever.

What must I do to maintain the edge of awareness, consciousness? To keep waking up? To deepen relationship to and in the inner life? Return to the experience of life within your own body, my teacher instructs me. Gently. Leave the mind's singular focus on the things *out there*, on the objects of its attention, and return to the breath that rises and falls. Let the breath see the world. Let the heart see the world. Return to compassion, to holding the essence of this life force with tender regard, as one would hold a newborn. Return to your intention, wordlessly or with articulation. Return to the very spot where you are. Return to the miracle of aliveness.

Unnecessary speaking, a subject that I know a lot about, is one of the primary ways to diminish the accumulated life force gained by inner awareness. Our *prana*, or life force, follows our attention, says Dr. Robert Svoboda, an author and distinguished ayurvedic physician. When our attention is captured by *anything*, our life force flows there. I often fail to keep the edge, therefore, because I am so busy discussing this or that, commenting on everything, filling in the empty spaces that are suffused with possibility, with the hollow sounds of my own self-importance. Early on in the gospel of St. Luke in the New Testament we hear a beautiful description of the inner life. After the birth of Jesus, when a group of shepherds arrives to bow down before the Savior—Christ the Lord—as they had been informed by a choir of angels, the scripture says, "everyone who heard it was astonished at what the shepherds said to them. As for Mary, she treasured these things and pondered them in her heart."(Luke, 2: 18-19)

The image of the Madonna and child—or of Claire and her unborn—is for me an image of silent containment. I really don't know that Mary was always characterized by this silence—she may have had a raging sense of humor, keeping her friends or family in delight with her brilliant repartee. Since the Christian scriptures aren't big in the humor department, her fun-loving nature has probably been overlooked. But, whether she was a comedienne or not, I do know that the archetypal descriptions point to her as *a woman wrapped in silence*. And I feel enormous power in that phrase; the words echo in my being as being true. I use them.

Keeping the edge of whatever it is I know, or whatever I remember, may be as simple and as enormously challenging as keeping my mouth shut. I know that my relationship with children, with my dear husband, and with my beloved guru is built solidly on a foundation of putting my attention on *them*, keeping my two cents (a right-on estimate of the value of most of my opinions) and my judgments to myself. From this place of silent attention, genuine sharing does arise. The heart does speak. Words are spoken. But these words bubble up from deep in the inner well. The words bind us at the heart, rather than separate or distract us. The deeper I drop into this well, the closer I get to the source, the groundwater that unites us all.

Dancing Our Way

> ... I revel only in the gladness
>   of my own welling love.
> In love there's no separation,
>   but commingling always.
> So I rejoice in song and dance with each and all.
>   —Baul song [5]

The Bauls of Bengal, India, are a sect of itinerant individuals and families of beggars, musicians and lovers of God. Traveling from village to village, and occasionally even to the streets of the great cities, they sing their praises and share the mood of their mystical relationship with the Beloved through their songs. The Bauls worship the union of Krishna and Radha, which is the union of the human and the divine, the male and the female, the transcendent and the immanent, the lover and the beloved, the body and the spirit. The Baul honors the body, respects its everyday miracles, and finds cause for celebration and thus remembrance in all its functions. Far beyond any mere notion that "this body is a temple" the Baul embraces the substances of the body that many have considered taboo or at least unclean and therefore unholy—menstrual blood, semen, even urine and feces. And while a more detailed description of Baul practice is certainly beyond the scope of this book, the question that such a cosmology provokes is worth considering for those who desire to walk an inner path.

How easy it becomes to keep my "spirit"-uality divorced from my human-ity. How easy it is to overlook the body as a source of wisdom, no less an altar for the mysteries of transformation. In my case, despite the perfection of the archetype of the pregnant woman, how easy it is to see this body as simply the vehicle of transport for the Divine, rather than the Divine Itself. And so many of the world's great religious traditions apparently support this "it's only the body" point of view. Even St. Francis of Assisi referred to "Brother Ass" when speaking of his body, although on his deathbed he asked forgiveness of this "brother" for his ill treatment. Such paradoxes can be mined for gems of wisdom.

Case in point: my own precious teacher—who espouses the Baul path with gusto—has consistently demonstrated to his students that the body's inclinations and cries for comfort have become our master. One year, as he traveled in India, he suffered from a foot infection that swelled his foot tremendously. Yet, he consistently refused to get medical treatment for it, and rarely stopped his breakneck pace to rest it. Another time he refused a disciple's offer of something to relieve some minor discomfort saying that as long as his disciples were lost in the need to attend to every burp or boo-boo in the body, he would not. Yet, in a mood of exaltation in which his body is a living prayer, he often refers to his own master Yogi Ramsuratkumar as the light that animates every cell of his body, causing it to radiate light and to sing unendingly the praises of the One.

Far from a call to indulgence and coddling, St. Symeon's declaration, the words of my own teacher, and the lyrics of Baul poetry and song testify to a rejection of poisonous servitude to the body in order to realize the transcendent mystery of freedom in the body. This distinction is critical. It takes a great deal of maturity and lived discrimination to see the difference between a brand of "practice" that will keep one imprisoned as it espouses the "my comfort first" principle as its core tenet, from one that flies freely within and without, using attention to and delight in the body as fuel for the ascent. The Bauls dance, they sing, they play a variety of musical instruments. Yet their music is highly refined, disciplined, trained over years of exposure and apprenticeship to the masters of the craft. The same is realized by any great artist—the work of Nijinsky looked both impossible and effortless, and we know it stood on a foundation of enormous discipline.

"As above, so below," the alchemist proclaims. "As without, so within," the Baul sings. And so the Baul practices seriously, with breath, with sex, even with intoxicants, with full involvement in but not "of" the world. Not because he or she wants to leave the body and float away into some bliss realm, but because the Divine is found here, now, embodied. The "man of the heart"—*maner manush*—is what the Baul calls this mystery.

It takes enormous discipline and exquisite guidance to walk such a slippery slope without succumbing to seductions offered at every rest stop, which is why the Baul also subscribes to the principles of guru yoga. Celebrating each of our senses as a doorway to the inner chamber, making everything holy, the Baul finds the Beloved in his or her heart, and is free.

Welcome to the inner life.

Mandala, colored sand and chalk.

31

The Development of Attention

We are caught by every vagrant breeze,
our lives a constant distraction from what is
right in front of us, our vision

always on tomorrow so that
we miss the glory of today.
But there are the few who understand

that the doorway to the Divine
lies in the cultivation of a present-Attention,
a facility for seeing what is

right in front of me.
Louis Agassiz, the Harvard naturalist,
was once asked what he had done

with his summer vacation.
I traveled far and wide,
he said. How far, he was asked?

I got
half way across
my back yard, he replied.

—Red Hawk [1]

— Chapter 3 —

Self Observation, First and Always

"How's it going?" my friend Jean asked good natured-
ly one day. In the midst of a particularly stressful work
project, I encountered her at the front entrance of my
teacher's ashram.

"My editing and writing work *is not* at the center of my
mandala!" I replied with passion, surprising both myself and
Jean. In the moment before the words flew from my mouth,
I had been having one of those rare, flash-of-insight moments. The interior considerations of many previous weeks
had coalesced in that one clear metaphor—the mandala.

"My devotion to God, my prayer, is at the center of
my mandala, *not* my business or busy-ness," I explained to
Jean, whom I knew would hear me without judging. "If I
can keep remembering this, everything else falls into its
rightful place."

Jean thanked me for the reminder. The image worked
for her too, she said, "I will use it." And, over many years,
sharing these simple words and this metaphor with others, I realize that it evokes a similarly powerful and grateful response. The question, "What is at the center of your
mandala?" is one that can guide a life.

The mind's preoccupation with the stuff of our lives,
and particularly with the theme songs of judgment and
self-limitation that play on the inner radio are major distractions, even roadblocks, in the inner journey. We all

have such theme songs, and that's not the problem. The problem is that we don't recognize how constantly we play them and how used to them we've become. You know the experience of hearing a song somewhere and finding that the song has stuck in your head? Sometimes it repeats for only hours, but often for days and weeks, until another one with a similarly powerful hook runs by.

Recently I read a book, called *Girls Like Us*, about three great female singer/song writers, Carole King, Joni Mitchell and Carly Simon. For days, at moments when I needed focus or silence, I found instead the "Circle Game" going "round and round and round" in my brain, only to be followed by "But will you love me tomorrow?" Reading a section about James Taylor, who married Carly in 1967, and hours later I was humming "Fire and Rain" as I walked through the grocery store.

We are all subject to such suggestion. And almost anything can trigger a familiar and related song. Bad enough when the song is a contemporary hit. Even worse when the "song" is full of our own lyrics of self-doubt, or a confirmation of our self-hatred. I know women who sing "I'm So Inadequate" in one of its many variations day in and day out. Others will sing "Growing Old" and "Nobody Loves Me," while my own personal favorites include: "Never Good Enough, Oh Baby!" and "Please, Please Like Me, Please." Of course the all-time greatest theme song, as far as I can tell, is called "Not Enough Love to Go Around."

The problem with such songs is that they wear deep grooves in the brain, and they take charge whenever the organism (that's you or me) is threatened. Singing them in the inner theatre, we soon start making our decisions based on such incorporated messages. We back away. We deny anything good that is offered us. We say *no* more than *yes*. We look for confirmation and affirmation outside of ourselves, hoping desperately to free ourselves from the grip of these inner monologue-monsters.

In fact, based on such songs, many of us are starving ourselves to death. Despite a tremendous outpouring of love and devotion, and even heroic work at times, sacrificing oneself for the greater Work, we aren't getting fed. We aren't eating the banquet that is laid before us. We are not picking up the treasures that lie along the sides of the road, begging to be used. And this is not only great stupidity on our part, but a great act of ingratitude. It might even be an act of consummate selfishness, I think, a type of spiritual bulimia and anorexia of the soul.

We might eat when we apparently have no other choice than to attend some spiritual feast: we go on retreat, we gather with likeminded sangha friends, we pilgrimage to a holy place … and so we become stuffed, temporarily, with the grace and blessings falling on us like leaves in a windstorm. Even though we might ask, "How can I maintain and nurture what I've been given?" we ask it without fully seeing the implications of such overflowing richness. To stay well-fed and satisfied in this domain might simply destroy the habits of a lifetime. It would undermine our self-definition and force us out of our tight little workout suits into some flowing blouse and skirt. It would change "God out there," to "Thou art my very self."

Some of my friends, holding to their repetitive songs of self hatred and unworthiness for so many years, are at the point of having their "spiritual"-stomachs surgically reduced in size so that they literally cannot take in the transformational blessings that are everywhere around them. They are about to walk away or at least back away from their practice, from their teacher, from their community of support. With this operation they *cannot* overeat. Not even a little bit. Intense pain of regret would be their feed-back mechanism.

When we talk incessantly of what is missing, when we don't stop long enough to establish even a momentary connection of relationship with someone near us, when we turn compliments into shit, when we replay our theme songs endlessly, it's no wonder we lack spiritual nourishment. Our constant NO to the force of life and our declarations of "not good enough" are turning us into skeletons.

In the New Testament we read the words of the man of faith: "Lord I am not worthy, but only say the word and my son shall be healed." This is a profound and mystical prayer when said from the domain of love. But, from the culture of self-hatred it is a mantra of death.

For now, reflect for a moment or two upon *your* favorite theme songs. Write them down, perhaps, if only their titles. Watch yourself throughout the course of a few hours, days, weeks, months. Observe how often and by what these songs are triggered. Appreciate that these theme songs are your own creation, based in faulty vision or judgment, or the result of family lyrics sung by your mother and father, which you naturally imitated from birth onward.

Is it any wonder that our inner life feels cool, unfocused, boring, when these theme songs are playing endlessly? And the part that is most sad is that we haven't self-observed to the point of recognizing that these songs in our heads are of our own making. They are certainly not the voice of a genuine lover (the essence of love within) telling us some secret. What a far cry from the invocations of gratitude that could be arising—moment to moment—from the heart; or the constant praise of creation, or the offerings of love and merit for the benefit of others.

A few years ago I met a radiant woman in her early eighties who has been a Sufi practitioner for over fifty years. In the midst of our conversation she casually noted, "What a great waste my life would be if I were not remembering God, the Beloved, with every breath."

It is never too late to turn back when we find that we're going in the wrong direction. Only rats in mazes "think" that they will get different results from doing the same thing that has never previously succeeded. We have to admit it when we find ourselves stuck. We have to stop long enough to recognize that we are in fact pressing number B-17 on the jukebox, again; that we are replaying our old theme songs just because they're tragically comforting in some perverse way. We might start looking at ourselves with "grandmother eyes." This means that we could take the view of grandmother to everything, and especially to our failings and habits and deep, deep patterns. Such are the eyes of compassion.

Only then might we recognize that we have a choice to sing a different tune. Mantra or prayer or breath practice is one different tune, and my elderly friend had certainly made that choice. Because she had practiced for years under the guidance of a Sufi teacher, she was able to give me a whiff of the sacred fruit of her persistence—a definition of attunement, a definition of conscious life, a direct means for linking the breath with the remembrance of God.

Know Thyself

At the risk of delaying your enthusiasm for *Igniting the Inner Life* I recommend that you read another book before, during or after this one. *Self Observation: The Awakening of Conscience* by Red Hawk (Hohm Press, 2009) contains the signature poem that starts this chapter. Red Hawk's book is a user's manual for the age-old teaching "Know Thyself." However, instead of talking *about* the necessity of self knowledge, which thousands of other books do, Red Hawk takes the reader by the hand and systematically instructs us in exactly *what* to do—that is, *how* to practice self observation, including exactly *what* to observe and why.

If I can encourage you, in the smallest degree, to admit that like me you are generally lost in this labyrinth of mind, asleep and dreaming, and unaware of your outer life (to say nothing of your inner life!), I will congratulate myself on a job well done. The brief observations that follow are strongly influenced by Red Hawk's work, together with those of my mentor, Lee Lozowick, whose teaching about mind, emotions and self observation is found in his book, *Feast or Famine: Teachings on Mind and Emotions* (see Bibliography).

To self observe—to "Know Thyself"—is the recommended first step in almost every system of self understanding leading to human maturity. Simply put, we start to monitor the contents of our inner awareness, our inner life. First we learn to "see" or feel or hear what's going on inside, instead of being run by these internal messages without our conscious knowledge. Sadly, however, the great majority of humankind is lost in some web of the inner life: tediously replaying conversations and events from the past, creating fantasies of what the future will hold, making plans to eliminate pain and to maximize pleasure, feeling enthused in one moment and fully depressed in the next, robotically buying the product seen on TV that morning even though not needing it, and all the while

noting and worrying about the twinges and burps inside
the physical body. More sadly still, they don't realize they
are lost. Either they don't know they are trapped in their
dreams and memories, obsessively treading air; or they
think, or even believe, that what happens "inside" is in fact
an adequate representation of reality.

Most sadly of all, *them* is *us*!

The second thing we learn about as we undertake this
practice of self observation is *not to judge* what we see, but
rather to simply become familiar with it. The idea here
is that our obsessive cycles of worrying, regret and self-
loathing are weakening not only our physical immune
system, but closing down those subtle channels through
which we might receive love, creativity and inspiration, as
well as a genuine remorse of conscience leading to transformation. Judging our processes and our thoughts adds
insult to injury, and keeps negative energy flowing in the
direction of exactly what we don't want.

Third, as we practice self observation we learn to bring
ourselves back to the simplicity of the present moment
and to live from there. We learn to live from the inside
out, rather than the way we have previously lived, which is
in reaction to any and every external stimulus that touches
us. No wonder the great religious traditions speak of spiritual *work*. Welcome to the work of the inner life.

Being Present

As we self observe we come to find that we don't live on
the spot where we are. We live in past or future (which is
actually the past too, as we simply project the past forward onto the path ahead of us and proceed to live into it).
When you can sense yourself *alive*, inhabiting your body

and breathing, located in space and time exactly where you are rather than in some fanciful past or future kingdom (or hell realm), you are present to yourself. When you sense yourself alive and breathing, and related to all other forms and expressions of life around you, you are present to *what is*. The inner life as I explore it here is synonymous with this sense of presence—an attunement to or awareness of your own spatial-temporal-body-mind-emotional complex.

"Being-presence" is the term used in some systems to describe this foundation of the inner life. Can you *feel into* what that means? Words are slippery when we try to explain such a highly personal phenomenon, but let's give it a try. Perhaps you've heard someone use the phrase "I had to pinch myself" in relation to some experience. Maybe you used it the first time you found yourself at the foot of the Eiffel Tower, or standing under the dome of the Sistine Chapel. There you were, seeing with your own eyes the familiar landmark or artwork that you'd seen in books all your life. But there was one critical and defining difference: you were *alive* in the physical presence of the real thing! So, quite naturally, you felt a sense of awe, or even shock. Like, "This is not a dream, this is not a picture. This is *it!*"

Or maybe you met some famous person, up close. Maybe you went to a rock concert and got to go backstage to shake hands with a celebrity you had idolized since you were thirteen. Or maybe you saw your favorite baseball star in an elevator, not two feet away from you. Or maybe you got to shake hands with the President of the U.S. I'd like that! I'd pinch myself too … anything to bring me more fully conscious of the fact that "I"—whatever "I" was—was actually here, now; and that this handshake was indeed happening to that "me." No fantasy, this was real.

Being-presence relates to these examples. But, instead of being directed to a person or place *out there*, being-presence relates to your own "pinch me, this is real" sense of your own being, your own aliveness. You are sitting on a bus and you *know* that you are sitting on the bus, and that *you*—not some fantasy character—are in fact breathing. You are alive and conscious, aware and present (they all mean more or less the same thing), inside your own skin. You are suddenly "congruent," that is, there is no ghost-image of yourself that hovers slightly off-center. With being-presence you are awake to where you are, and how you are, and where your attention is located. Attention located within *and* without, with no incongruence ... being-presence! Attention casually and unconsciously flying around the room, or roaming the past, or projecting into the future ... less chance of being-presence, unless you happen to be carefully observing the change of location of your attention and are present to that change as it is taking place.

These two qualities, being-presence and attention, are foundations of the inner life. Men and women who live *from the inside out*, therefore, are men and women who always know where their children (their many potential and wandering "I's") are. Men and women who live from the inside out are not easy marks for every distraction that whispers an invitation.

Attunement To What Is

If you have ever cared for children, your own or someone else's, who know that children often get a "groove" going and don't want to be disturbed in it. Maybe they have a fullscale play-dough bakery in operation, or maybe they are digging their way into the neighbor's yard, or maybe their dolls and stuffed toys are enacting the drama of the littlest mermaid. When an adult with an adult agenda enters this magical world (as in, "It's time for dinner," or "We've got to leave now") the once-humming groove suddenly turns into cacophony. Tears, screams, complete ignoring, or resistance and refusal are common reactions to the invasion of a groove.

Life itself has a major groove as well. The planets turn in it. The day and the night dance to it. And events proceed within it. Earth is in that groove, but that doesn't preclude the occurrence of hurricanes or mudslides. Remarkably, however, except for the unconscionable interventions of human greed, the Earth maintains itself within the groove. Learning to slow down long enough, or relax deeply enough, to hear or feel the hum of the human groove in relationship to the Earth's groove, and the Universe's groove, well, that's a good description for what I mean by attunement to the flow. The *Tao Te Ching* uses the metaphor of a river. It flows, it changes direction, but whether it flows over sand or around boulders it is still river, being river-ly, true to itself, doing its river thing.

This *going with the flow of life* is a state of relaxed *attunement to what is*, as it is, here and now. It is this hum of the flow that one settles into with a regular meditation practice, which is one of the primary ways whereby we reignite the inner life and keep it burning. That hum is also the language in which God speaks. In a theistic context, the man or woman who is living and listening with open ears to the hum, is the man or woman who is living "the will of God."

A woman once asked my guru, "How do we know the will of God?"—to which he replied that God was speaking this will all the time, and we just had to listen. When the woman inquired how she was to know it was actually God speaking and not simply her own fantasy, he said rather wisely, I thought, "You just have to learn God's language."

> This all is a great Mystery that has no answers. The answer is to Be Ignorant, Be Impeccable, Be Happy, and know God, Who is This Great Mystery. The answer is to do what is needed, what serves, what heals, what is sourced and fed by Divine Influence. The answer is to not allow innocent curiosity to turn into a poisonous demand for answers or no-Work. The answer is to relax, breathe deeply, and go on about the Will of God, which is inherently and tacitly obvious (if one is relaxed and not bound by the tension of "why?").
> Answers in this business are not static and final. They flow with the circumstances, the Divinely Influenced needs of the moment. —Lee Lozowick [2]

One who practices being-presence leaves behind the clutter of the mind's preoccupations and begins to develop the habit of attention. Practice in the habit of internal attention is the same as taking a course in God's language, because God speaks in everything. But usually, because we are so disjointed and distracted, we flail about deciding if the correct response is *Bonjour* or *Hola* or *Guten tag* or *Namaste*. There are so many conflicting languages racing around in our heads, it is no wonder we feel confused about what to do next.

My guru once noted that every life situation offers one and only one *optimal* response. The man or woman living the inner life is more likely to be aligned with that optimal. Your own experience should bear this out. You *know* the feeling of being in the flow. Athletes know it, commonly. In that groove they make basketball shots that could never happen under ordinary circumstances. In that groove they simply see where the optimal move is, without the logical mind having to discuss it. The decisions and activities of our outer life, when informed by this type of inner listening, are more likely to be established within the groove that the Earth is in.

Take a moment right now to stop and observe: the posture of your physical body in space; your internal sense of aliveness; the labels you are placing on the "emotional" energy that is circulating or pooled in one spot; your facial expression; the quality of your breathing (don't try to change it, simply note how it proceeds); where your thought attention is romping about; what is going through your head … and simply allow it all. Now, stop yourself four hundred times before lunch today and do the same. Get to know yourself.

A Shift of Context

Self observation allows me to see that I can go away for three weeks or three months of isolation, accepting my loneliness, devoting myself to prayer and practice on retreat, or a vision quest, or whatever, and still, even though I may be getting up at 4 AM or spending twenty-four hours chanting the name of God, I may be doing nothing more than rearranging the deck chairs on the Titanic, as we noted in Chapter 1. We might expend a lot of effort, and even feel good that we have established some order in the midst of chaos, and yet the ship of our own inner life has hit the iceberg of ego's co-optation, and is going down. Nothing we are doing is having any real effect on the bigger picture.

We are making ourselves feel better, but we're on our way to a cold and watery grave nonetheless.

Most of us, and myself heading this list, are still contextualized by "the world." This doesn't mean that the world is something bad. It is not to be equated with sin, or even with self-indulgence. But it is the herd mentality; the culturally conditioned and learned mindsets and values that we have been indoctrinated with, and which we reinforce on a daily basis. For example, I am held in place by an old worldview in which I am the elder sister, the first child in the family, and don't even notice when I act out this role to keep everything in place and peaceful within the family. Or, very strongly in my case, I am held in place by an old worldview of having been a Roman Catholic nun. This brings with it a huge set of expectations, and the most admirable ones are kept and polished to gain the strokes and attention that I so desire. My worldview may inspire behaviors that are kind, generous and compassionate, but still they are based in the context of building up a persona that the "old world" will approve, thereby assuring acknowledgement for my goodness, wisdom and service.

What to do? The practice of self observation answers that. There *is* nothing to do about one's enmeshment in a world context except to be clear and open-eyed about it. To accept it, to say YES to what is, without judgment, is the only way to make any opening in the barrier of ice around the heart. And our enmeshments *are* that—they are ice walls that buffer us from genuine feeling. To deny such observations, or to fail to examine oneself at all, is to stay in a fantasy, much like the deck-chair-arranging scenario. The ship of ego is going down, but we are "doing good things" that are essentially irrelevant, yet thinking they need doing.

The context of the real work-on-self demands that we see what we are up to. Not in order to find ourselves blameworthy, but rather because the work of genuine transformation, which is not other than "Know Thyself," is about being free to move, to respond, to choose, without the unconscious or subconscious chains that keep us in place as per the world's assessment of us.

Over time, seeing how mechanical and self forgetful we are, we may simply and naturally find ourselves responding differently. We may gently and simply break an old pattern, not because we should, but because self integrity demands it. The choices may be large or small: "I can't come home for Christmas this year," may be one way that our self honesty shows up; or "I'm not buying that, because I don't really need it!" or "I'm not eating that ..." We might even find that we are ready to say "I'm not a victim!" as the shocking result of seeing ourselves swept along in the unconscious tide that has ruled our world since early childhood.

If, for me, I am not practicing awareness of the context I presently support, and renewing my aim toward a shift out of unconscious, mechanical life ... well, I might as well start drinking up all the most expensive wine in the ship's bar. But:

> Here's some good news. This is extremely good news. Any moment that you can remember to ask yourself, "What is my aim?" in that piece of a moment you are awake; you are awake. Where the subtle impulse meets the physical mechanism of the brain, so that it arises in your consciousness, "What is my aim?" at that infinitesimal, invisible meeting of the subtle impulse with the physical awareness, you are awake in that moment.   —Lalitha [3]

A Meditation Practice

"You either have excuses or you have results," said somebody, at some time, and that somebody might very well have been a teacher of meditation. Without some time spent in simply sitting still, developing awareness of what's going on inside, listening to the endless tedium of my theme songs, seeing the habits of emotional defense that keep me wandering aimlessly through the supermarket of past hurts and future kisses, I have nothing but excuses for my fragmented, unconnected existence. I'm lost.

The crazier the world out there becomes, the more essential it becomes to stop—or at least *see*—the madness within. Meditation practice is no longer an option for any of us reading (or writing) this book. Postponing self observation until tomorrow will simply postpone it forever. What about now? Now! Now!

I know you think you have good excuses for why you can't *fit in* a meditation period today. Please forgive my heavy handedness here. I'm talking to myself, as my excuses are really solid! But, I've simply learned from long experience that without this stabilizing factor of a time for doing nothing but self observation—observing whatever it is that arises in me—I'm adrift. But what's worse, without self observation I'm fully identified with this drifting dream. Whether it's the dream of being the best or being the worst, I actually *believe* that this is who I am, that I know myself. I therefore keep the game going—maintaining the façade of the personalities and fantasies that earn me the most points with the most people.

Our world needs to stop. My world needs to see what it's up to.

Keeping quiet

Now we will count to twelve
and we will all keep still.

For once on the face of the earth,
let's not speak in any language;
let's stop for one second,
and not move our arms so much.

It would be an exotic moment
without rush, without engines;
we would all be together
in a sudden strangeness.

Fisherman in the cold sea
would not harm the whales
and the man gathering salt
would look at his hurt hands.
Those who prepare green wars,
wars with gas, wars with fire,
victories with no survivors,
would put on clean clothes
and walk about with their brothers
in the shade, doing nothing.

What I want should not be confused
with total inactivity.
Life is what it is about;
I want no truck with death.

If we were not so single-minded
about keeping our lives moving,

and for once could do nothing,
perhaps a huge silence
might interrupt this sadness
of never understanding ourselves
and of threatening ourselves with death.
Perhaps the earth can teach us
as when everything seems dead
and later proves to be alive.

Now I'll count up to twelve
and you keep quiet and I will go.
　　　　　　　　　　　　—Pablo Neruda [4]

Who first, if not me and you?

~

Other books and numerous teachers of meditation have
instructed you in what to do, so I'll not repeat them here. I
will, however, draw one distinction that may prove beneficial. Meditation or self observation practice as I'm talking
about it here is not about visualizing a heaven realm, or
a life of perfect peace, or a meadow of flowers in which
you meet your spirit guide. That's another task, perhaps,
another type of practice. Here I'm urging all of us to stop,
much as Neruda begs, long enough to observe *what is*, and
to simply watch the mind, learn its patterns, and emotions'
manipulations, and recognize that these patterns of mind
or emotional energies are arising in you, but that they don't
define you. You can also think and feel excited about visiting a zoo without mistaking yourself for an armadillo, can't
you? Our thoughts and emotions are the inhabitants of a
vast inner zoo. I can look at them, enjoy them or not, but I
don't ever have to climb into their cages.

49

The Summer Day

Who made the world?
Who made the swan, and the black bear?
Who made the grasshopper?
This grasshopper, I mean—
the one who has flung herself out of the grass,
the one who is eating sugar out of my hand,
who is moving her jaws back and forth instead of up and down—
who is gazing around with enormous and complicated eyes.
Now she lifts her pale forearms and thoroughly washes her face.
Now she snaps her wings open, and floats away.
I don't know exactly what a prayer is.
I do know how to pay attention, how to fall down
into the grass, how to kneel down in the grass,
how to be idle and blessed, how to stroll through the fields,
which is what I have been doing all day.
Tell me, what else should I have done?
Doesn't everything die at last, and too soon?
Tell me, what is it you plan to do
with your one wild and precious life?

—Mary Oliver [1]

— Chapter 4 —

The Prayer Alternative

I have laid mandalas on the rocky soil at the entrance to my teacher's residence in northern Arizona for a long time as a form of physical and visual prayer. I began the process in the mid-1990s after returning from India, intrigued with the rice-flour patterns—known as Rangoli in the north and Kolam in the south—that Indian woman traditionally lay out at their doorsteps. Some sources have explained that this practice, typically done by the senior woman or women in the household, originally had immediate and practical value. The rice flour attracted the critters (insects, rats) from within the house, drawing them away from the living spaces. Other writers have indicated its meaning within a village culture; the rice flour design was an indicator that the family within was well. Without a freshly swept yard and freshly laid pattern, the other villagers knew that the household was preoccupied ... with sorrow? ... or sickness? The art, or lack of it, was a morning news report.

The mandala—a circular pattern which underlies the art and ritual in practically every world culture—is clearly a microcosm for the unfolding pattern of my life. The center of the mandala in Indian art is called the *bindi*, a reference to the infinitesimally small spot at the center of the universe from which all creation emerges. Sort of a black hole in space; or the source point for the "big bang."

51

Interestingly, the same word applies to the tiny dot of vermillion that an Indian woman colors on her forehead, at the spot between her eyebrows—the "third eye."

My own experiments in Kolam art were primitive, at best, as I labored with wheat flour, finding that its consistency was difficult to work through my hands. The Indian women, and their girl children who practice from the time they are quite young, are fully adept at the art. They stand, bend from the waist, and swirl the flour through their fingers, releasing it in a thin line. Using a grid of dots, which they lay out first, they connect the dots or encircle them to weave designs, sometimes of great simplicity, an unfolding flower perhaps; sometimes of elaborate detail—a ceremonial cart complete with candles and peacocks, with the image or symbol of a presiding deity at the center.

Despite setbacks of skill I persisted. I really wanted to learn this art, and more than that, I wanted to do something beautiful, something that might delight my teacher and other sangha members. Most had been to India, some numerous times, so I knew that this artwork would carry special meaning for them when sighted on our home soil. I also wanted to do something that connected me with the web of creation.

Over years I've worked to create mandalas with powdered lime mixed with powered tempera paint; with masa harina and corn meal, and actual grains of rice. One year a friend decided to help by grinding up colored sidewalk chalk in her blender, which turned out to be a bad idea. I used marigold petals with gorgeous results, but our garden marigold population was quickly depleted and I managed to create a lovely pattern only three-feet in diameter.

At last I discovered colored sand, in a wide variety of colors, and since then my mandala-art life has taken off!

Now, five times a year, I spend four to eight hours in one day in a type of active prayer—laying out a large, delicate and colorful pattern to signify a particular holiday with significance to my community of friends, and in celebration of my guru. And, other women have stepped forward to assist me, as this mandala making appeals to their desire for a contemplative art practice.

The work is hard, requiring lots of bending, and the weather in our northern desert environment can be sizzling or blustery, even with layers of protective clothing. But the practice is joyful, as it serves as a tangible reminding factor—a representation of some cosmic principle that applies directly to our lives. It encourages me to stay focused, to repeat the Name of God, to keep offering the mandala as my contribution to the sacred mood of the celebration.

The Life of Prayer

Literally, *mantra* comes from two Sanskrit words, *man* (*manas*) meaning "mind" and the suffix *tra* meaning an "instrument or tool." To use mantra is a powerful way to stay at the center of the mandala, to keep the mind and heart on track, protected from the insidious mind parasites of fear, illusion and scarcity. Saying the Name of God, whether that name is Jesus or Allah or any other, is a powerful practice for these historic times. In the Indian cosmology, as I noted previously, we are currently living through the kali yuga, an eon in which the forces of darkness are triumphing. Many Indian sages advise that the use of the Name of God, in any number of mantric forms, is particularly valuable in these times. We need this compass to keep referring back to, as the distractions of materialism and the gloating voices of the victors (i.e., the demonic forces) are calling out to us everywhere.

I admit it! In this kali yuga, like my family and friends around the globe, I've convinced myself that I'm too busy to take time for longer and more intensive practice. This is why mantra, particularly saying the Name of God, is so valuable, and so necessary. In one of his recent journals, my teacher Lee Lozowick put it this way:

> In the Kali Yuga ... we practice various disciplines with as much enthusiasm, will, ease and attention as we do, and still, at the end of the day, what we're really left with is the Name ... This is the ground upon which we walk, or could be. This is the rocket that lifts us into space to explore the "outer limits," or could be. This is, as the Indian Scriptures call it, the boat that takes us to the other shore, or could be. This is our nutrition, our deep feeding, or could be. This is the vehicle of our Blessing, the Harmonization of our lives, the peace of our minds, the balancing of our karma, or could be.
>
> ... [W]e begin the use of the Name for whatever reason, good, bad or indifferent (Sattvic, Tamasic or Rajasic—the orders don't align) and as we practice, even rote, empty repetition, it is the power, force, and Divine radiation of the Name Itself that subtly, and occasionally miraculously or Mercifully or dramatically alters the mood and reason and intention of the practice. We will, not we might, but we will, as long as we maintain some minimal continuity in the practice and use of the Name, find that our entire relationship to it changes, begins, again slowly, but in some cases

with alarming speed and intensity, to take on the aura of something we not only enjoy but actually anticipate, long for, feel overwhelmed, in a most positive and even ecstatic way, by. The Name itself entices, entrances and even entitles us. It captures our hearts and makes us fall in love with It, with God, maybe even with It's creation, holy Cow, holy Smokes, holy Holy of Holies! [1]

Mantra is one form of interior prayer. And prayer, as I have written of it previously, "involves us in the mystery of God, love, life or truth, demanding of us both action and surrender. To pray is to cultivate a love affair with love itself, the most awesome power in creation." [1]

The old Baltimore Catechism that I grew up with in the Catholic Church defined prayer as the "lifting up of the mind and heart to God." A good start, I believe, but a bit lacking in remembrance of the body's role in the process. Prayer, I think, can be expressed through mind, heart, emotions and the full extent of the physical body, whose energy field apparently never ends. I can pray by dancing and dishwashing; I can pray by being silent in the cathedral at midnight mass. As long as my intention is directed toward *that* which mysteriously permeates creation, I'm in prayer.

Prayer for me is the occupation—actually the preoccupation—of the inner life. It can be a means of waking up the "deity" or the essence that sleeps within; a way of consciously remembering where I am and what I'm doing here; a means of offering myself, and all my thoughts and actions, for the benefit of others; well, the list could go on and on. But, the point remains that we have a choice about who or what sings within.

As we continue with our explorations of the inner life, we will consider these foundations of prayer and remembrance from many different perspectives. For now, the important thing is to orient ourselves in the direction of not wanting to waste a single breath. Or, as the poet Mary Oliver says in her wonderful poem *The Summer's Day*, which opened this chapter:

> ... Doesn't everything die at last, and too soon?
> Tell me, what is it you plan to do
> with your one wild and precious life?

Begging at the Feet of Love

Enormous interest in and re-dedication to prayer has only increased over the years since I wrote *Praying Dangerously*. In that book I attempted to make a case for adult prayer—the case for spiritual maturity in relationship to God, the world, and the things of the spirit. Urging readers to consider that prayer could so easily become routine, childish or fantastical, I offered what for me constitutes the essence of both the inner life and the life of discipleship—a willingness to die to self in order to live for God, or Truth, or a Universal Reality, whatever term best applies.

It had become obvious to me that the popularity of prayer, as evidenced by the vast number of books written on the subject each year, was both good news and bad news. Good news in that more people were coming forward with their hunger for deepening or expanding the inner life, and bad news because prayer was being treated like a commodity—a new market to be milked and thus saturated by perhaps well-meaning people, but confused and full of illusions, who hoped to use this current interest for their own popularity or profit. I offered my views to counter this spiritual materialism.

A sentimental view of the things of the spirit is one that is dependent upon good feelings, signs, everyday miracles. Nothing gives away the naiveté of the practitioner like the magical thinking of the child: "Oh, God always gives me the perfect parking place" or "Oh, God held off the rain just until my marriage ceremony was over." The distinction here is that of the childlike versus the childish relationship to life. The difference is between awe and natural wonder, on one hand, and magical thinking in which everything revolves around me. Prayer that asks God to change the weather to suit my plans, or even prayer that begs for an end to the fighting in my home is still reminiscent of an all-powerful hand guided and manipulated by those who put the most money in the collection basket. What the childish sentimentalist does is restrict the Divine, and the fiery nature of the spirit, to one aspect of a particularly common fairy tale. God's workings for good are limited to those that further *my* plans and move the flow of history in a direction that I deem appropriate.

With this immature view in mind, however, I know that I painted the picture of petitionary prayer a bit too simplistically. A few readers, men and women I respected, all but apologized to me that they still prayed *for* things. That feedback shocked me, and I experienced remorse for my lack of clarity on this point. Then again, I'm on this path for the same reasons they are. At this turn in the road I understand much more clearly that not everyone who begs "Lord have mercy," or "Father forgive them for they know not what they do," is relating to God as Santa Claus. The 13 Indigenous Grandmothers who travel the world as ambassadors of peace urge everyone to pray, as they do, and each in her own way. And, many of the prayer forms they demonstrate are forms of petition, forms that place the human in the dust, bowing down and imploring Infinite Mercy, Infinite Compassion.

The Grandmothers Mission Statement

We, The International Council of Thirteen Indigenous Grandmothers, represent a global alliance of prayer, education and healing for our Mother Earth, all Her inhabitants, all the children, and for the next seven generations to come. We are deeply concerned with the unprecedented destruction of our Mother Earth and the destruction of indigenous ways of life. We believe the teachings of our ancestors will light our way through an uncertain future. We look to further our vision through the realization of projects that protect our diverse cultures: lands, medicines, language and ceremonial ways of prayer and through projects that educate and nurture our children.[1]

Humans are … well, just that, human. Because we have bodies, we *have* needs, even if we consciously work against enslavement to these needs. Humans do terrible things to other humans. Circumstances prevail in which suffering rains on the just and the unjust alike. Children die as a result of fetal alcohol syndrome or sexual abuse. If our cries for mercy and our broken-hearted laments are not to be included in the bibliography of prayer, well, it just doesn't seem right to me to say that God is everywhere, and in all things. I stand corrected.

When it came to the use of petitionary prayer, I noted that all was well and good provided we added the caveat that Christ used, "Nevertheless not my will but Thine be done." But, I see now that few of us may be at that point of surrender, yet, even if we aspire to it. Now it is more useful for me to view petitionary prayer as an attempt at alignment with God's own infinite qualities. Therefore, I can beg for mercy, patience, kindness, fierceness, integrity … remembering and waking up these qualities within myself. Or, for those non-theists, remembering and waking up the qualities of the *bodhisattva*, the embodiment of compassion, within me.

What I now see as useful petitionary prayer is the offering of a cry to heaven in which we beg the manifestation of God's own being in ourselves (although such descriptions are terribly anthropomorphic). We beg God's mercy, then, not as some outpouring from the sky, but rather as the opening of the channel of mercy that already exists within us. We beg for healing, not in the context of God as the pill fairy or the benevolent doctor of heaven, who will magically reach down and turn the tumor into a ball of golden light. And while that visualization is certainly a valuable one, the cosmology of God it represents smacks of childish dependency. Rather, our cry to heaven in this case is the urgent outpouring of a body-mind that has temporarily lost its relationship to *its own healing wisdom*. You can probably relate to this phenomenon that happens when you are sick—you tend to disassociate and even to loathe that part of the body in which the pain or problem lies. Our prayer, then, is our attempt to align with the source and reality of healing itself—namely, with the life force that inhabits us! We are the repositories of the life force; and we have billions of years of cell wisdom to guide us.

A mature relationship to God and prayer is obvious when we feel called to pray on behalf of others. In February 2008 our community received a notice in the form of a letter written by the guru, in which he told us that he had been diagnosed with inoperable cancer. Needless to say the news came as a serious shock to the body-mind. What does anyone *do* upon hearing such news about a loved one except to recognize that "his" mortality was terrifying because it reminded me of my own, and therefore inspired me to prepare for death. But also, I felt that prayer was being called for. But what, but how? The exact approach to such prayer was unclear to me at the time.

And so I waited, forestalling any sudden action and definitely not wanting to interfere with whatever healing- or prayer-process he had going on in his own being. For several hours I merely watched the thoughts and emotions and physical sensation of numbness and weakness that rose and fell. A short time elapsed, but then I got the message: I must interject none of my own intentions into this delicate alchemical mix. The very best thing I could do, I realized, was to make the intention of aligning with his intentions, and offering the energetic and devotional "substances" of my heart to him, as additional support or strength. Was he "praying" for God's own clarity and vision to be awakened in himself so that he knew whether he should work diligently at some healing regimen or not? Was he "praying" for God's own courage to endure, or simply for the faith and clarity of his own guru, Yogi Ramsuratkumar, who declared time and again that "Father in Heaven is caring for this body," embracing death with complete surrender? Was he praying in alignment with the Divinity that animated each of his children and closest loved ones, that their courage, strength and clarity be quickened?

I think I have a better understanding of prayer now than I did in February '08. Being able to make this distinction between "praying with" and "praying for" was useful to me. Perhaps it will be also useful for you. And further, this distinction between begging for something "out there" as opposed to quickening what is already "in here" has served me tremendously, as my natural inclination to cry to heaven now has a firmer foundation; a more mature grounding.

---

28 Definitions of Prayer— in the style of Carl Sandburg

Prayer is the lifting up of the mind and heart to God.

Prayer is the longing for merger with the source of Love, enveloping mind, heart, and the full extent of the physical body, whose energy field apparently never ends.

Prayer is an ocean into which we sink, celebrating with wonder the marvelous sights and colors of bubble and fish.

Prayer is the pool of God into which we plunge, ready for anything.

Prayer is the communion with the most interior sense of self, and the recognition of that interdependence with all other life.

Prayer is aliveness in God; with eyes always open.

Prayer is a cloak of clouds, descending over the shoulders and enveloping the whole being in the silence of what is.

Prayer is the ache of the great expanse of the barren desert, awaiting the rain of God.

Prayer is the cry of the heart, acknowledging utter pain, confusion, helplessness and begging for mercy.

Prayer is a song sung from the top of a mountain at sunset, in praise of the vanishing day.

Prayer is the pull to the light that greets the sleeper at 3 AM, begging to be acknowledged.

Prayer is the coolness of a mountain spring, to a dry and desiccated heart.

Prayer is a slice of radical self-honesty served on a banana leaf and offered to the feet of the Divine Mother.

Prayer is an annihilating fire, burning the dross of old leaves accumulated in the corners of one's life.

Prayer is the frozen crystal in the dead of winter receiving the first rays of morning sun and beginning to drip.

Prayer is walking up the hillside with the name of God spoken at every breath, and a sense of vigilance on the lookout for snakes.

Prayer is a hurricane sweeping through the soul's office, blowing important work papers across the desk and onto the floor.

Prayer is the spontaneous arising of compassion and the dedication of merit upon hearing of a most recent horror in Afghanistan.

Prayer is witnessing and blessing the beauty of children.

Prayer is stopping, paying attention, and remembering.

Prayer is breathing, and knowing that "I" am breathing, and letting that breath stand as witness to the marvelous miracle of the process of life in me.

Prayer is embracing the loved one and not moving away too quickly, allowing energy to begin
to flow as one between you.

Prayer is the wordless gasp of awe upon encoun-
tering beauty.

Prayer is the acknowledgement of the empty
hand and the empty heart, and the willingness
to stay empty.

Prayer is stepping into the chamber of emptiness
and finding it suffused with compassion.

Prayer is. All things pray. All things pray by their
very being in response to the life force.

Prayer is petition, supplication, praise, thanksgiving, and adoration and purification.

Prayer is the complaining, the defending, the
justifying, and the arguing before the door of
God's mercy.

—Regina

The Living Prayer of My Guru

Of course it is not politically correct these days to have a
guru. Such a one is seen and written about as being ludi-
crous at best, dangerous and even deadly at worst, with
little tolerance in-between. Still, I have one, and have had
the same one for twenty-five years. I am deeply grateful for this. The ebb and flow of my own life—the contrast between the contracted heart versus the heart that is
transformed into a vehicle of prayer and praise—reflects
the fact that I can turn to my guru, a man of deep prayer,

who praises God from morning 'til night, regardless of the circumstances that surround him.

My guru does this invisibly, and even with smoke-screens covering his life of inner contemplation. He calls his inner life "the bluebird in his heart" (a reference from a Charles Bukowski poem) and he refuses to talk about it, or let it out. He knows that the context of the world is such that tender devotion is crushed by the machine of spiritual materialism and the thousands of tiny bastions of the "religions of one." But, for those who have the eyes to see, his inner focus upon the core of loving-kindness, compassion and generosity, together with his ceaseless praise of the One, is not hard to discern.

My guru is a heavyweight, a fact that challenges me day in and day out. He will not be satisfied with anything less than my complete alignment to what is. Like the vow of stability taken by monks in a Trappist monastery, my heavyweight guru anchors me to one place, one path, one tradition. He drives the car along this road of the inner life. My efforts are as necessary as the gas in the tank.

One who is anchored can float a bit without fear of drifting too far. And, truthfully, this anchor has never re-stricted *anything* that was real. It has sometimes appeared to limit the amount of ocean surface I could traverse—in much the same way that any commitment to enter in by one door naturally closes others; it would be a travesty to choose marriage and remain "single"-minded at the same time. But, this anchor has demanded that I explore the depths over which I float. Yes, that's the essential point— the essence of prayer. Prayer brings me to the awareness of the *depths* over which I float. I am connected to those depths, no matter what I'm doing on the surface.

Jai Guru!

Mandala, colored sand.

"Honor, soul, heart" … all we really mean is
    "the Beloved."
All we really mean is *This*, the rest isn't worth all that.

All this fire and tribulation, pain and affliction
    only point to our Beloved
or else all this lecturing and scribing is not worth all that.

To the whole world Hafez has become a Beloved.
With the Lover though, name and fame
    isn't worth all that.

                                                —Hafez

                            ~

If my head could imagine
how happy my heart is with You,
the wise would trade their wisdom
for the chains that bind me to You.
That Grace your beautiful countenance has revealed
puts this graceful beauty in every line I write for You.
                                                —Hafez[1]

                            ~

How can one who is Aflame at the bottom of an ocean,
be still?
                                —Sheikh Abol-Hasan[2]

Chapter 5

The Art of the Heart

For many years I've been privileged to meet with groups of people, particularly women, who are interested in prayer or spiritual life, or the lives and teachings of the great masters and awakeners. Whether the group happens to be in Des Moines, Iowa or in Bucharest, Romania, the first fifteen minutes of any talk or seminar inevitably results in tears—sometimes shed by a few, occasionally shed by many.

The reason for this response is predictable, and I've taken to keeping a box of tissues at hand for the deal. My introduction to these participants, similar to some of the introductory passages here, is to remind them of what they already know and what they are longing for, and thereby allow them to again *feel* and *know* the love that infuses it all.

And so they cry—unexpected tears of joy, of relief, of tender appreciation, and also tears of blessed remorse for the many long weeks, months and years in which they've kept themselves distracted from the reality of who they really are. Moments of such remembrance are precious. While they may not fully anchor us in the ocean of love as the context for all that is, they do serve as points of reference. A meditation practice or a prayer practice or a practice of serious self observation forge this anchor and lower it.

Unashamed

I am essentially unapologetic in my stand for love! (Although I almost never verbalize that stand, as it makes too many people uncomfortable. Better to just *be* the love, than preach the love.) If I am completely misguided in my claim, so be it. I accept responsibility for having made a fool of myself in the eyes of the world. If love is *not* the one all-pervasive reality, consciousness, force, God, Goddess, truth ... well then, oops. Is your alternative a better one?

Ah, but what if I am right? What then? Yes, what then? One of my favorite quotes, this one from Samuel Taylor Coleridge, reads:

> What if you slept
> and what if, in your sleep you dreamed
> and what if, in your dream you went to heaven
> and there plucked a strange and beautiful flower?
> And what if, when you awoke you had the flower
> in your hand?
> ... Ah, what then?

Yes, what then? What would your life be like if you were convinced and soaked in the recognition that *love is*? What would your relationships be like if you *knew* that the "love out there" was not separate from the "love in here," and what if you knew this about the presence of love in your partner, your kids, your parents, that person who predictably seems to make your life miserable?

What might be different if all your decisions were made from this contextual ground of love rather than the ground you have staked out and are living on up until now: that ground called "it's a jungle out there," or "gotta protect what is yours," or "eat, drink and be merry because ..." or "I'm not good enough," or "this job is killing me," or "what about *my* feelings?" You can easily continue the list, if you want to. It is endless and can be endlessly personalized. The ground of "not enough love to go around," otherwise known as the ground of scarcity, is enormous. Its possibilities are limitless, and its suffering is incalculable.

And now? This moment? This day? What if? What if in that next phone call you *knew* that love was not scarce. What adjustment might you make then? Or more accurately, what adjustment might naturally unfold from that knowing? Recall the words of Kahlil Gibran: "And think not you can direct the course of love; for love, if it finds you worthy, directs your course." [3] Yes, what if!

What if, in the moment you caught yourself obsessing about some future scenario—job, family, physical health, whatever—you were suddenly reminded that you were not separate from the love that governs, creates, sustains and completes all that is? And, what if you simply decided that it was more delightful to move your attention to *that*, locating its abiding center (although you know it is everywhere, still you often experience "it" as emanating from some center within your body) and resting there?

And what if, in the midst of a conversation with a difficult co-worker, or a solid wall of resistance in some job-related task, you were to fall into the mind of God, the heart of love, the remembrance of what is? What then? Ask this question with me, now, and perhaps walk through the next hour or so asking it again and again. I will be doing the same. Let us journey together on this pathless path, in love, direction: Love.

This exploration of the inner life is a pilgrimage, as much as any trip to Bodhgaya or Lourdes. At each rest stop there is a signpost to remind us of how far we've come and how much further we have to walk. But, instead of listing this in terms of physical distance, these signposts contain questions to move us from the outside in. They invite such reflection as: What is going on *in* your body right now? Where in the body does this sense of self abide? Is there any emotional overtone to whatever is present? Are you relaxed? Are you breathing? Let the breath be love. Inhale … exhale.

It is important not to grasp at what's been remembered here. Let it go! Trust me, the trick is in the letting go. It *does* come back, fresher and stronger. The grasping and the attempts to hold it, and the design of circumstances to get it back will *kill* it. Let go of all the wonderful, radiant, blissful memories and simply rest in what is. Lean forward into what is, what is, what is. No judgment.

Doctor Goodheart

I have a doctor whom I see once or twice a year. He is an osteopath (D.O.) by training, which is good because that allows many people to use their medical insurance in seeing him. But, despite his legitimacy in the eyes of the state, he is no traditional medical doctor. For our purposes let's call him Dr. Goodheart.

Dr. Goodheart is so busy that generally you are told that you need several weeks or even months to get an appointment. Furthermore, if you call for the first time, his secretary will report that he is not accepting new patients. Nonetheless, don't hang up. I've rarely heard of anyone who didn't get to see him within a few weeks of their call, first-time patient or not. "Oh, wait a minute," the friendly receptionist may tell you, "we've just had a cancellation. How about 3 PM today?" And, 3 PM just often happens to be the only free slot in your otherwise sealed-in day.

The oddest thing about visiting Dr. Goodheart is that there is no medical apparatus of any kind in his office or treatment room. No sink, no rubber gloves, no stethoscope, no tongue-depressors, no leaflets explaining the advantages of this drug or that. Just the tall, thin, gentle-faced doctor sitting in a chair, and you (fully clothed) sitting on the treatment table. You talk, he listens, and then he stands behind you and lightly places his fingertips on your skull, or the back of your neck, or knees ... it depends upon what your complaint has been. He then makes an adjustment—maybe he presses on one of your ribs, or pulls your head up slightly so that it aligns more with your cervical vertebrae, or does a little rubbing in the area of your knees.

"There," he says, "that should feel better in a few days." Surprisingly, despite the fact that he hasn't caused any pain, and that his whole "adjustment" session took less than two minutes, I'm often on the verge of tears by the time he is done. Some vital force has suddenly been restored, or renewed, like a faucet has been turned on and the once-parched soil is surprisingly cooled. *What just happened?* I ask myself, and him. But, he doesn't bother to explain much, except perhaps a vague reference to relieving some of the pressure on the *frammelsats* ... or something. "Oh, good," I tell him through my tears.

I am in love with Dr. Goodheart, the way I imagine people fall in love with those who rescue them from alpine snow caves or solitary beaches on islands in the Pacific. He never fails to bring me back among the living when I didn't even realize that I was walking around comatose.

71

As I take a moment to let his adjustment sink in, I open the conversation with him about how to keep this energy moving. "Have I introduced you to the Laws of Healing?" Dr. Goodheart asks of everyone. Old and new alike, every patient leaves his office with the same prescription in hand, a small business-card bearing the words "Law of Healing." Below the heading, these magical words: "I will heal if I listen to my heart."

"Take some time every day to repeat this law to yourself," Dr. Goodheart advises. "Meditate about it. Think it over. This is the answer. Come back and see me when you feel the need."

"Well," I ask, "should I keep up my usual vitamin regimen?"

"Whatever you need."

"Should I take the trip I was planning next week, or stay home and have a long rest?"

"Do what your heart tells you."

"How long before I can play tennis again?"

"Oh, you'll know if you listen to your heart. Good-bye." No time to linger around for useless pleasantries, as Dr. Goodheart has an office full of clients waiting for their ten minutes of attention.

Someone whose opinion I trust deeply once told me that Dr. Goodheart is not a doctor but a healer. In fact, it is his unqualified trust in the wisdom of the heart in each of his patients that makes him the miracle worker that people honor him to be. He has one message, and he can deliver it powerfully, along with the skillful means of his osteopathic profession, because he has lived it himself for thirty or forty years. He lives by the direction of his own heart, and anyone who comes into his presence with a grain of sensitivity is affected by this pure and highly

intentional energy. And that's why so many keep coming back to get another hit from the heart-doctor. And
that's why so many experience almost immediate relief
of their symptoms, but sadly recreate the situation that
caused these symptoms in the first place after a few weeks
or months.

But, Can We Trust The Heart?

Telling this story about Dr. Goodheart in a weekend seminar, I asked the women to consider whether they thought
his prescription was right or not?

Some of the women immediately objected to the overly
simplistic nature of his directive. "It could just be an excuse
to do whatever you damn-well pleased!" one particularly
tight-lipped woman declared. "How do you know which
voice is the heart and which is just the self-hating critic?"
objected another. The type of inquiry they were doing was
precisely the reaction that Dr. Goodheart's medicine was
intended to provoke.

One shouldn't *think about* the wisdom or naiveté of
Goodheart's words too much, I explained. Rather, I suggested, they'd be better advised to simply notice what happened inside themselves the first instant they heard this
story—before the logical mind had the chance to counter with why it could never work. This bodily knowing,
this awareness of the intuition of the heart, is fabulously
described in Elizabeth Gilbert's *Eat Pray Love.* Here she
talked freely about her relationship to a guru, right now in
the twenty-first century, and in one significant section described her relationship to an ancient Sanskrit text known
as the *Guru Gita* which was recited daily on her guru's
ashram in India and elsewhere. I was cheering, applauding

her skillful means in writing in such a way as to inform the general public (our Catholic or Jewish mothers and grandmothers, no less) about a branch of practice that was hitherto completely foreign and probably even antithetical to them. "Right on, Elizabeth," I said out loud. Most exciting, for me, was her story about her ambivalence for the *Guru Gita*—this ancient text recounts the love between Shiva and Parvati, guru and disciple. She was bored by the daily chanting. She resisted it. And yet, against amazing odds, she found herself being drawn back to it, again and again. Her story is a paradigm for how *the body knows* what it should do, what it wants, and what it needs, regardless of the mind's resistance. She was using her relationship to this practice as a way of affirming that the logical approach to existence was not necessarily the best one available, in any dimension of reality.

> It may be that when we no longer know what to do we have come to our real work and that when we no longer know which way to go we have begun our real journey. The mind that is not baffled is not employed. The impeded stream is the one that sings.   —Wendell Berry[4]

Along similar lines, Dr. Goodheart's methods are written in a code that addresses the heart, the place of intuitive wisdom, deeper than the mind. His approach to healing is a faith-based, love-based one. He works at the level of healing the energetic body and empowering the essential wisdom of each patient. For those who take his prescription seriously, Dr. Goodheart's methods have sometimes proven more powerful than radiation or chemotherapy. Those who have asked the question, "What does my heart want?" with extreme candor, have initiated a journey within that often resulted in a miraculous cure, but more likely generated a healing at all levels. They have found that the question, "What does my heart want?" is the same question as, "What is the truest aim or ultimate purpose of my life?" It is the same question as "Who am I?" And in our case here, it is the same question as, "What is the inner life? And how shall I re-ignite it?" And, in living with this inquiry they have reordered their lives, reclaimed their own compasses, and released the limiting beliefs that have kept them sick and tired, and unhappy.

A Path With Heart

> Anything is one of a million paths. Therefore, a warrior must always keep in mind that a path is only a path; if he feels that he should not follow it, he must not stay with it under any conditions. His decisions to keep on that path or to leave it must be free of fear or ambition. He must look at every path closely and deliberately. There is a question that a warrior has to ask, mandatorily: "Does this path have a heart?"   —Carlos Castaneda[5]

I first encountered this quote by Carlos Castaneda more than thirty years ago. And you? I recall the shiver of recognition I had when I first found it, and how I copied it immediately into my journal. Over many years it has been one I have returned to with interest and passion.

Early on in my spiritual journey, I honestly thought that I understood the question, "Does this path have a heart?" Thinking back on the immature ways in which I took this very refined piece of wisdom, it was sort of like asking a four-year-old child, "What do you *really* want to be when you grow up?" Granted, some four year olds *do* know, and manage to create a life for themselves to manage it. But most don't. Most want what appeals to a four-year-old imagination—ballerina shoes and flimsy tutus, fire engines and blaring sirens and high-power hoses, space ships and laser swords.

As a senior adult I read this quote with awe once again, but this time I notice a phrase that rarely got my attention back then. The phrase is "free of fear and ambition." Only then, Castaneda says, will the warrior be able to make the correct decision about which path has and which path does not have heart.

Does anybody else see the dilemma here? To be free of fear … well, let's get real here. Who among us can lay claim to that? And to be free of ambition … well, to my understanding "ambition" equates to desire of any kind. Anybody ready to testify that he or she is free of that?

How is it that I may have read this path of heart quote dozens if not scores of times and never before found that this phrase stopped me? Probably because I thought that merely saying, "OK, *if* I were free of fear, what would I choose?" or "*If* I didn't give a damn for ambition, what would I choose?" and that fantasizing helped me, right on the spot. *Good deal!* But now, as I approach the issue again, and hopefully with greater maturity, I have to ask myself these questions with a new level of urgency. I have to ask ruthlessly, yet compassionately, and then answer them with a harder truth—namely, that I am still obsessed with fear, and still run by desires, and that these fears and desires are often unconscious. They may be programs I got when I was an infant, like the fear of loud noises, or the fear of spiders; or desires that I got from MTV; not even mine, when I examine them closely. Nonetheless, they possess me because they are thick in the air I breathe in twenty-first-century USA.

To say "follow your heart" and leave it at that is a platitude that makes a lot of money for a lot of greeting card companies. Sadly, it is akin to putting a tiny band-aid on an extruding broken bone. To learn God's language—to learn to listen to and live from the heart—is a worthy intention, and one that requires enormous commitment, practice and time. I for one don't merely want to pretend to be "free of fear." I for one don't merely want to fantasize being "free of ambition." I want the *real deal*. Consequently, I've put all my eggs in one basket. Call it the path of Know Thyself. Or the path of Truth. Or the path of God's Will, or the path of Love. Whatever you call it, without a blazing inner life to fuel it, the path is not a genuine path of heart.

"Love is letting go of fear," the *Course in Miracles* suggests. My teachers have instructed me that in returning to the source place of love *within my body*, fears are more readily seen for what they really are. And "I" am less inclined to identify with them, or give them attention.

Devotion

The cultivation of devotion is one of the most powerful and effective ways of nurturing an inner life. However, the mere mention of devotion can raise a problem for some because of its overtones. Have you seen it—the phenomenon that happens at rock concerts or football games? The spectators are sometimes so overcome by passion and so aroused by emotion that they lose their sense of self, along with restrictions to propriety. The result may be wild dancing, screaming, flailing about, or fighting as a means of release or the expression of ecstasy. In these moments we are witnessing a variety of devotion—that ardent, often selfless dedication to a person or a principle.

Another *rasa* of devotion that we may have some familiarity with is the romantic and sentimental relationship to a religious figure or a spiritual entity. The devotee who walks in the guru's footsteps picking up the stones that the guru's feet have touched, saving these same stones as the most precious jewels … well, such a one may be so lost in love that their fervor takes a form close to madness. Certainly if we read the lives of many great saints of all the religious traditions we *do* find this degree of devotion. When it's real, it can be inspiring, or even frightening. When it's imitative, it's childish and cloying.

In either case—the football game or the darshan—the devotion expressed may be so alien to our sensibilities that it is cause for fear or ridicule. We may unconsciously (or very consciously) determine that *we will never* lose ourselves to this degree. Fear of such intensity may cause us to erect barriers to pure feeling or ecstasy in its many expressions. Fear of losing control may lead us to cynicism, to intellectualism, to avoidance of any situation that even vaguely promises such possibilities, real or not. What it boils down to, I think, is that we are afraid of the madness that love may contain. Avoiding situations in which love may burn out of control enacts a high payment within our souls.

A group of my friends perform an original rock opera, called *John T,* about the many dilemmas present to the character of St. John the Baptist. Among other venues, they take the rock opera in an abbreviated version to nursing homes during the Christmas season, as a means of entertaining the residents. Usually their audiences are octogenarians, or men and women severely afflicted with dementia. We're not sure that these spectators are getting the message of the production, but we know they enjoy it. Their faces, their clapping hands, their tears of recognition when Jesus or John step on stage tell us so!

At one of these institutions a few Christmases ago a severely crippled younger woman attended the show. Confined to a wheelchair, with all her needs attended by her caregivers, she was bright, alert and smiling during the performance. Speaking afterward with the actor who played Jesus, she held the man's hand, looked deeply into his eyes, and thanked him for his work. "It is so important to be swept away," she said with passionate sincerity.

I agree. And yet I know that some of us are more naturally oriented to being swept away than others. Some of us, admittedly, are bliss junkies. We *feel* with the intensity of a forest fire. Others do not. External coolness, or what a "hot type" might term "emotional blankness or numbness," is not necessarily a sign that the hunger for the spirit is lacking. The hunger may be taking another form—even a highly refined form. After all, we learn from our theistic mystics that the love of God is not about emotionalism. In fact, the hottest fire might be the one burning at the depths of the ocean. And our Buddhist teachers will instruct us that the nature of reality is emptiness, suffused with the cool nectar of compassion. Or maybe our longing is temporarily obscured. Maybe it is being protected, and for good reason. Who is to know?

All that said, I still dare to suggest that the cultivation of devotion is one of the surest means of loosening the hard-packed soil of the soul. I also dare to suggest that one doesn't have to *feel devotional* in order to benefit from devotion, in much the same way that one doesn't have to *feel* naturally attracted to one's children or grandchildren all day long and every day in order to still care for them, serve them and bring them delight. We serve our children because our genuine love is bigger than our loving feelings. We serve them, and in the act of service itself we are softened, drawn in, even melted. Slowly, and yet inexorably, we are won over. We see. We are touched. We learn the ways of love. So, maybe we grumble inside; but when the choice is ours, we make it with integrity. We *act* with love; we express our devotion because it is the right thing to do. Love, it seems, is the cosmic law, whether we feel loving or not.

My spiritual teacher says that we can't *make* devotion happen, but we can practice obedience to the obvious will of God. Our gentle embrace of the work of raising our children, aiming toward clarity and compassion, is the foundation from which devotion arises. As we nurture our aim by remembrance and attention, we are transformed. And so are our children. Such love aligns us with the transcendent.

We hunger for the ultimate—whatever we name it— regardless of the complaints of our small minds. To cultivate devotion, then, does not mean that we have to violate what we imagine is our authenticity. For me, cultivating devotion starts with the recognition of what I am *naturally* delighted by; of what naturally leads to some up-leveling, a sense of the sublime within my life. Whether that delight is flowers or music or the face of a child, or the profound silence that surrounds me when I enter the meditation hall, or the welcoming smile of the saint, Anandamayi Ma, who laughs at her children's drama and seriousness— I cultivate devotion when I make this association a part of my life on a regular basis. Therefore, I nurture friendships and circumstances that will encourage me to stay close to the sources of my delight. When I accept and celebrate that love has an infinite number of faces, I nurture the devotion that is unique and precious to me.

My friend Jake is a rationalist and something of a curmudgeon who rails against the devotion that others take for granted in relationship to God or guru. Yet his tender heart encompasses a broad spectrum of humanity. We might laugh at or be frustrated by (depending on the day) his predictable complaints, his self-deprecating humor, or his objections to whatever way the prevailing wind is blowing. But, for those who know him well, no bluster can fully hide his heart of devotion. When Andrea, a mutual friend, was stricken with serious illness, it was Jake who volunteered his time generously, above most others. His service was gentle, unassuming and reliable. Thus, the form of his devotion was sculpted with his hands and feet, with sweat and dedication.

Nevertheless, the tragedy for Jake, as for so many of us, is that he suffers unnecessarily. Like me, he falls victim to his own thoughts, judgments and opinions about himself. Thus, he denies his love. He denies his devotion. He frets about the past as if it were tangible, and projects these chimeras into the future. He fails to inhabit his body, or this moment, instead choosing to re-tell (and believe) the story of alienation that has become a lifelong calling card. He turns from the beauty of his own tender and longing heart. Jake might never (on his own) conceive of putting this beautiful and longing heart on the altar and bowing down to it. He might never imagine that becoming devoted to himself would be a way out of prison. Nor would he entertain the possibility that the "Constellation Jake" is a figment of imagination, and that the truth of genuine heartfulness, love and devotion is the ground of being in which "Jake" has arisen.

It is by seeking to know oneself that the Great Mother of all may be found.   —Anandamayi Ma

Certainly some wise person has said something like "show me what you are devoted to and I will tell you who you are." It is the same as saying, show me what you are willing to obey; or show me what you are willing to bow down to; or show me what you are willing to sacrifice to or for; or show me what uplifts your heart and expands your boundaries; or show me what sweeps you away. And, while some of us might be tempted to dismiss such expressions as they appear at rock concerts or football games as somehow "beneath us," we might be wise to reconsider that something valuable about the inner life, the quickening of the flame, may be contained here. We might decide to start looking at the world as a theatre of devotion, finding it everywhere. Learning from it everywhere.

The "children of this world" are wiser in their day than are the "children of light," said Jesus enigmatically, and I've always loved the FULL STOP this brought about in my usual evaluations of things. These children of the world—whatever their focus—are passionately dedicated to their cause. They are willing to throw aside what anybody else thinks of them. They obsess about the object of their devotion—whether it is their beloved rock idol or their nationalistic pride. And they will sacrifice time, energy, money and even their lives to prove themselves worthy of association with their god.

If my life temperature remains essentially lukewarm, fear is winning out over love. Unless I'm willing to examine the dullness, and embrace it in the present moment as the immediate "what is" of my life, I'm not going to be able to move through it. Face it with gentleness and hold off the judgment. See it everywhere. Then, each time you do, re-articulate your aim. This is the best way I know of to warm things up.

I also know that it helps to take a pilgrimage. I can start by walking across the field that adjoins my home. I say I am devoted to the Earth, so how about taking up the challenge of crossing this field with that devotion in my feet, in my legs, in my lungs? I can also pilgrimage to the lunch table with the same type of devotion. Food is God's body; can I receive it as I would eat Holy Communion? I can take a journey, with aim, to the feet of a wise elder, and place myself as an empty vase ready to be filled with whatever flowers this one may offer. I can enter an exquisite garden, visit a temple or monastery, spend a few hours in a hospital nursery, or simply open a book of devotional poetry (like what Rumi writes to his beloved Shams E-Tabriz) and savor each sensation and each word with reverence and even awe. Expanding my boundaries just a little bit, I am oriented again in the direction of my aim. Putting myself in the vicinity of people, places and things that encourage devotion, it rubs off.

Ultimately, I can entertain the sense that whatever forms I am using—Earth, food, guru or teacher, garden, child's face, friend's arms—are all pointing in one direction, to the truth of non-separation. This constellation of energies that I limit by the name of "Regina" is really not separate from the love, the beauty, the tenderness, the power that surrounds and penetrates me. Chipping away at the ice of fear that protects what I think is my center, I find nothing but emptiness suffused with Mother Compassion.

I enter this temple of emptiness and bow down to Her there. She has *my* face, because She has every face.

The Creative Art of Heart

I recall my first trip to the Rodin Museum in Paris in the late 1980s. I entered the room in which Camille Claudell's small sculptures were displayed alongside those of her mentor (and lover), Rodin, and my legs got so weak that I had to find a wall to lean against. My breath became a panting of sorts. I thought I might faint, or kneel down and kiss the ground—one or the other. The effect was beyond all conscious control.

Just as great athletes know something profound about the power of attention, artists know something profound about following the directives of the heart. In this case, "heart wisdom" is synonymous with "body wisdom," as its communications don't necessarily proceed only from the energetic center in the middle of the chest. As happened to me in Paris, I feel the communication of great art in my solar plexus, which at times will start to vibrate without any conscious direction. Sitting at a concert, I never know when the spirit may strike. Sometimes I'm surprised by what initiates the fluttering.

I also know when I have created something that has proceeded from the inspiration of the heart (or the body): a line of poetry, the answer to a child's question, an elegant meal, an intricate mandala. I know that the heart is at work because I feel deeply satisfied, fed by the *process* even more than the result; and regardless of the small flaws that exist in everything, I am pleased. Occasionally I get confirmation from outside that others have appreciated the work too. But, ultimately, I'm not working for that. I'm working because the heart's substance is a necessary nutrient in the diet of my soul. Without it, served up regularly, I starve and dry up.

"Are you nurturing your art?" I ask my friends. Not surprisingly, so many of them have excellent excuses about why they aren't or "can't." And, their inner lives are starving as a result. Not only that, they tend to get sick, driven by stress that saps their creative life force. These friends are not untypical of the culture at large. The messages we get from everywhere are not heart messages. Instead, even when we are urged to exercise, or practice our music, these directives come from a context of dryness and survival, not a context of juiciness and love. I've seen the exercise classes at the local gym. I've asked myself why these women (or men) don't look happier, despite the fact that they are using their bodies in what could be ecstatic movement. I've also attended writing workshops and asked the same thing. These folks are often intent on publication, *not* on writing as a source of inner life nourishment.

For years my friend Kelly kept her painting apparatus piled in a dark basement. Every time we spoke I begged her to get it out and start painting again. She had fine excuses for why she couldn't, but always promised to look into it. She also had a divorce to handle; child custody to battle for, and debilitating depression to deal with. Why couldn't she see the connection here, when I saw it like a whale washed up on a beach? She was out of her element and trying to make it work.

I'm happy to report that after years of denying herself, Kelly is not only painting but sculpting, designing the interiors of shops and offices, and making gorgeous jewelry. She is also healthier than she has ever been. What about you?

When I am not doing my art, I am drying up. My art may be as simple as a weekly trip to a flower shop, followed by an hour spent in making interesting arrangements for placement around my house. My art includes making mandalas. My art includes reading and writing poetry ... poetry I will never publish! My art includes writing, a few hours a week on the weekend, and as often as possible in my journal. My art includes making a pot of fine green tea every morning and savoring it in a small porcelain cup as I watch the day break.

When I am not "doing" my art, I am starving.

If the connections are not yet clear enough, look up "art therapy and cancer" on the Internet and read the stats. I actually found this delightful statement in an article posted by the University of San Diego Medical Center, Moore's Cancer Center: "Some neurophysiologists report that art, prayer and healing are all associated with similar brain wave patterns and stem from the same body source. Art therapy's proponents believe that the creative energy stimulated by the project contributes to the healing process." [6] Well, of course. Doesn't it make sense?

The work of the inner life is the work of transforming impression food into a substance that can feed the Divine, or the ongoing love that drives the universe, or the building and maintenance of soul. It doesn't matter how we language it, there is necessity in igniting the inner life. Necessity not only for ourselves, but necessity for the well-being of everything and everyone with whom we are connected.

Mandala, colored sand.

The Guest-House

This being human is a guest-house.
Every morning a new arrival
A joy, a depression, a meanness,
some momentary awareness comes
as an unexpected visitor.
Welcome and entertain them all!
Even if they're a crowd of sorrows,
who violently sweep your house
empty of its furniture,
still, treat each guest honorably.
He may be clearing you
out for some new delight.
The dark thought, the shame, the malice,
meet them at the door laughing,
and invite them in.
Be grateful for whoever comes,
because each has been sent
as a guide from beyond.

—Rumi [1]

— Chapter 6 —

Barriers to the Inner Life

"He who looks outside dreams, he who looks inside awakens." —Carl Jung

Sometimes the best way to talk about what something *is* is to determine what it is not. And since I'm attempting to make some useful distinctions about the inner life, to look at those attitudes and beliefs that temporarily douse this inner fire or discourage its blazing may provide a useful source of inquiry. What follows are nine such distinctions, each of which I have struggled with over the years. Many of which I still do.

1. Perpetual Motion

"Just stop, Regina," I said to myself as I took seat 13D on the airplane to Nashville, on my way to the National Headstart Conference where I was promoting our company's children's books. "Just stop. Do nothing for a while, and give yourself a chance to remember where you are and what you're doing here."

But, let's face it, there were so many things to do that promised a known and immediate gratification. There was that blueberry scone from Starbucks to be eaten. There was an airline magazine to be browsed for Sudoku puzzles. There was my recently acquired novel that promised to be so terribly engrossing, yet to be read. There was even more work to catch up on, or this book to be developed in my journal.

When my choices are listed here in black and white they don't seem all that wondrous. But in the moment they were absolutely absorbing. In fact, they were so fascinating that their alternative, to silently stop and to do nothing so that silence might arise, seemed paltry in comparison; even useless, stupid.

You know how fascinating those 10,000 things can be. You know how many times in a day you take the easy, the immediate, the more predictable route to occupy your time and attention, and all the moreso when you are not at your desk or in your kitchen doing something that *has* to be done.

I propose that the urging of the inner longing ... or the pull to see more deeply and express that in prayer or gratitude ... the urging of the heart, is rarely silent, and can in fact be heard, but only when or if we are willing to stop, look and listen for it. In dozens of ways, all day long, this call to listen is heard. I've often thought that the Muslim practice of stopping throughout the day, five times, to remember God and to literally bow down, was one of the most beneficial acts that a human being could do. To recontextualize the moment; how remarkable!

We Could Stop

We would stop if we *had* to. We all know that, because we have done it. A death in the family? Watch how quickly things can be rearranged. How many unbreakable deadlines can be fluidly adjusted or excused with the urgency of crisis. If you were racing along the highway at 80 miles per hour and you suddenly sneezed hard, momentarily causing your glasses to fly off your face and onto the floor of the car, you would probably slow down and pull over. Or suppose you suddenly experienced a sharp shooting pain down your left arm accompanied by intense waves of nausea. I bet you'd drive onto the shoulder of the road as soon as you could.

External signs are sometimes so unquestionable that we are forced to heed them, otherwise we know we will suffer more serious consequences. But most of our warning signs, like those of mounting stress, are much less compelling and immediate. A shortness of breath, perhaps; a tightening in the lower back; or that growing impatience that leaves us snapping at people who approach with a simple question—these we get so used to that we tend to overlook them, and fail to notice their growing frequency. If only we would STOP at such times, regroup, self-examine, breathe, make the next move into conscious attention … if only if only if only.

Since we disregard such obvious physical cues or discomforts, can we actually develop a greater sensitivity to the movements in the soul? Or, to put it another way, can we attune to the channel of inner wisdom or prayer (like those traffic conditions broadcast on FM 411) which delivers urgings and warnings and inspirations all the time?

The poet Jane Kenyon speaks about what I'm pointing at in a poem called "Happiness":

There's just no accounting for happiness,
or the way it turns up like a prodigal
who comes back to the dust at your feet
having squandered a fortune far away.

And how can you not forgive?
You make a feast in honor of what

was lost, and take from its place the finest
garment, which you saved for an occasion
you could not imagine, and you weep night and day
to know that you were not abandoned,
that happiness saved its most extreme form
for you alone.

No, happiness is the uncle you never
knew about, who flies a single-engine plane
onto the grassy landing strip, hitchhikes
into town, and inquires at every door
until he finds you asleep mid-afternoon
as you so often are during the unmerciful
hours of your despair.

It comes to the monk in his cell.
It comes to the woman sweeping the street
with a birch broom, to the child
whose mother has passed out from drink.
It comes to the lover, to the dog chewing
a sock, to the pusher, to the basket maker,
and to the clerk stacking cans of carrots
in the night.
It even comes to the boulder
in the perpetual shade of pine barrens,
to rain falling on the open sea,
to the wineglass, weary of holding wine. ²

One never knows when the upwelling of the heart's
wisdom will arise. But, the question remains, will we STOP
long enough to give it space to spread its roots or to blossom? Writing these words I am reminding myself that the
heart is signaling me to stop, look and listen all day long,

and in dozens of ways—from noticing a flower in the path, to noticing my judgments about the person sitting next to me on the flight. I remind myself that I can STOP, *now*, despite my arguments to the contrary.

> Sick unto death, we will be stopped,
> and as we moan, perhaps in agony, we will decide
> to slow down and live, at last.   —Regina

When my task is more important than the person I push over in my path, I am too busy. When I'm unable to maintain relationship within myself, with a child, or with another adult, I am simply too busy! Busyness is a selfish excuse for an unlived potential.

> Western people are running from themselves and they use the *busy-ness* of their lives as an excuse to *avoid having to actually live their own life.* We are terrified of who we actually are, terrified of the inner space that is the basis of human experience … By being busy you are basically giving away your human existence.   —Dr. Reggie Ray [3]

Age-Old Wisdom

"Don't just *do* something," the master directed his disciple, "Stand there!"

The disciple—who happens to be a friend of mine—still repeats this injunction to herself, daily, after more than twenty-five years. Still, she is plagued with the itch of accomplishment, with that need to prove her worth and wage her private war with decrepitude and death. Her energy is vital—strong in her gut and solar plexus—even as she is well into her fifties now. Like so many of us, she is blessed and cursed with this type of "just do it" energy. The blessing is that she creates wondrous art, a beautiful sanctuary home, and several large-scale projects that serve children in her community. The curse: that unless she is vitally employed, she doubts her worthiness. Sitting still, she is planning what's next, next.

The inner life suffers from our attempts to rush it, and unfortunately the literature of spiritual transformation feeds the sense that whatever "it" is that we are supposed to be able to accomplish—like recognizing *the power of now*, for instance—can be done quickly, even instantaneously. After all, we have *really* important work to do, don't we? Shouldn't we be teaching, or at least giving workshops, or writing a book, or something?

In stark contrast to this impatience for "doing," my teacher's spiritual Father, Yogi Ramsuratkumar, who commonly referred to himself as "this beggar," once told this story on himself to his disciple Perumal Raju:

> Once some missionaries had come to see this beggar and they said, "We Christians are doing real service to humanity—building hospitals, schools, orphanages, etc., whereas you don't do anything!" What to do, Perumal Raju? They are saying like this, what to do! Does the Sun build hospitals Perumal Raju? Does it run schools? Build orphanages? But because of the sun, everything happens! The Yogi is like that!" [4]

"Living in perpetual motion" is another way to speak of this detour in the inner life. We could also call it "half-baked prayer." It all stems from the same sense of impatience that is endemic to the culture in which we live. Not surprisingly it infects us inside and out. We don't want to live a *life in process*—we want a diploma and a new assignment! Our desire for instant gratification is one of the most deadly desires we can harbor if our aim is the building of a soul, or the cultivation of an inner life. "Deadly" because it rushes to fill the chasm of inner longing with anything that will ease the sensation of hollowness or emptiness. And emptiness is *exactly* what the inner life needs as its foundation. A weekend workshop that promises to turn you into an *avatar* fills the inner chasm with cement. "Good for you" it extols, seductively. "Now go on out there and share the truth with everyone!" Whether it is rocks or shiny trinkets, the tendency is to fill-in-the-blanks with whatever is closest at hand, rather than endure the sweet agony of insecurity, of not-knowing, of being always in process.

My guru uses the dictum "No top end" to describe life with him. He cautions me that there is no arriving, no being finished, no graduation. I've been in his company for over twenty-five years now and he is still brand new and surprising to me. (I am brand new and surprising to myself, and so is the life of silence and prayer in which he has immersed me.) He could just as well say, "No bottom end," which he has too. Unlike the single-focused work of the journeyer into the underworld—the one who has to retrieve the golden ball or the magic staff, whatever—the wayfarer in the inner life as we consider it here finds the ball and merely touches it, thereby opening a hidden cave into which she is now compelled to dive. And the journey continues.

The man or woman who would cultivate the inner life would celebrate a sense of never being satisfied, and allow themselves to rest peacefully in that. He or she would sing and dance to the music of "on and on." Holding one's place without dissipating the energy of attention, or longing, or love, the inner chasm would be widened and deepened. Then, with even the faintest whisper of prayer or praise, its walls will echo.

> ... it's a mistake to hasten the unfolding of spirit. I've always developed with great difficulty, very slowly, the spirale (spiral curve) of my soul is very tightly wound up and unwinds at an inexorably slow pace.   —Nikos Kazantzakis

The desire to leave the hermitage and get busy in order to save the world is the great temptation of the monastic. And such a temptation is only solved by a changed world vision—an appreciation of the entire field of conscious-ness, often called the Mystical Body of Christ, in which one knows that every organ and cell in the body is vital in doing the task it has been given to do. When we disregard our own calling, like the care for our children, to rush into the marketplace or into battle, we are violating a principle integral to the inner life. Understandably, when the heart opens, the energy swells, the light explodes all around, the love wants to be expressed in some way. It wants to embrace everyone with outpouring love, and this is no problem. When it wants to leave for Africa and start a mission for AIDS babies, leaving one's own babies, there is some contradiction here. Yes, such love wants to give back to creation what it has been given. And for many of us it wants to do that actively, with a title attached. This has always been a torturous part of the journey of the contemplative. This wanting to run out screaming "I love you" from the rooftops, leaping over the walls and throwing himself or herself into some ministry. It is such a burn to … *burn*. Yet, this burning might just be the alchemical fire that produces transformation in the soul, and food for God.

Today, let us consider how intensely love and life burns. How terribly, heart-wrenchingly real it is, and how we are drawn up and out of ourselves to both meet it and to reciprocate. And, let us simply burn. There is so much "self"-interest that makes one's love sticky, and the great ones tell us that we have to be smooth and clear to enter the kingdom of heaven. Otherwise, if we are half-cleansed we will go out and do the same things we've always done. We'll let things adhere and then we'll start adjusting them so they look nice, and before you know it we've got the Me-Myself Charitable Trust for Women and Girls going.

Of course we could conceivably wait around for too long, I suppose, and never share the love that is brewing in the inner vats. A character named Poor Judd in the musical *Oklahoma* apparently had this problem—he supposedly had a heart of gold, but never let on! Instead, he was mean and nasty to everybody around him. But I'm not talking about becoming like Poor Judd. Truth is, if one *really* stays in place and loves creation, loves God, loves people … a great gift is offered to the field of consciousness. And, amazingly, like a magnet drawing iron filings, seekers and those in need are drawn to one's door. The ways and means of dynamic service are shown to us; handed to us in fact on a silver plate. Much of the rest is ego deciding to "do good" rather than simply "stand there."

One could die, I think, empty of all except a heart ragingly on fire, and such a life would be a great contribution.

2. Going It Alone

I'm not good at driving late at night alone. I live at the edge of the grid—no highway or street lamps—and have to travel long stretches of two-lane road where the speed limit is 70 MPH. At midnight, heading back home from a gathering of friends, I play loud music and sing or chant to stay awake. Still, I've scared myself once or twice with a minute swerve that sent me onto the shoulder of the road. There is no margin for error out there.

Going it alone is another of those unspoken and rarely questioned foundations of our cultural milieu. And, to its credit where the inner life is concerned, going it alone *should* be understood as a necessity. On the other hand, and the all-too-common hand, the banner of "going it alone" is more frequently waved by those who categorically disavow surrender and obedience to anyone or any thing besides their own inner voice.

The trouble is that any position *against* outside help, and/or any crusade *for* going it alone is extremely risky, if not utterly foolhardy. When it comes to climbing Mt. Everest alone and without a guide, it amounts to sheer idiocy. Sure there have been individuals who made the ascent alone, and some without supplemental oxygen. *And*, some of the best of them have become disoriented from altitude sickness and made a critical error of judgment that resulted in not only their own death but the deaths of those who attempted to rescue them.

The telling factor here, on Mt. Everest and in the inner life, is that unconscious influences (like the need to prove something to a domineering father) kick in when the air gets thin and the thinking-mind muddled. At 20,000 feet, after a night alone in sub-freezing conditions, the climber who has dropped one of his gloves or his goggles often doesn't even know that he has dropped one of his gloves or his goggles. He or she simply accommodates and pushes on, or lays down to sleep, or decides to jump off the cliff. He or she simply doesn't know that they are seriously impaired in all their faculties. A companion, a guide, or another climber encountered on the trail who points out the impairment may mean the difference between life and death.

The explorer in the inner domain can also become seriously confused or deluded. "[A]nd following the wrong god home we may miss our star" writes the poet William Stafford.[5] And the voice of the heart, that voice still and soft within, while itself essentially true, perhaps, can also be easily distorted or co-opted by unconscious factors—the need to be perfect, or regret for past "sins" are not the least of such unconscious motivations.

In other places in this book I'm pleading the case for listening within and for eschewing that external standard that has us all jumping through hoops. But, without diminishing these pleas in the slightest, here I will beg you to consider the value of the companion, guide or witness—who can be our sangha mate, our husband or wife, a wise elder or friend—and ultimately the blessed advantage of the teacher or the guru on the path. After all, most of the great ones—saints, saviors, gurus, buddhas—have had one or more companions or teachers. The desert fathers and desert mothers of the early Christian hermetical tradition practiced devotion, surrender and obedience to an elder. Even in the rare instance that the younger monk's realization was more advanced than the mentor's, he or she embraced surrender and obedience to the spiritual mother or spiritual father as much as possible.

Like that rare Everest adventurer who has made it up (and down) alone, there have been solitaries and saints who have broken away from their superiors and even their traditions. They have risked all—sometimes resulting in death—to follow that inner directive, the voice of God. Witnessing their lives, however, or reading their words, we often discover that they claimed to have no choice. They weren't holding to "I did it *my* way," in the Frank Sinatra sense of things. Rather, because they were in obedience and surrender to the One, they were *taken* to the next level, often sadly bemoaning the fact that they must leave their guides behind.

One who is so consumed by the inner fire that she is thereby blown like seed to new ground is in the midst of a transformational birth-labor. One who decides that she is "beyond the need for a teacher or group," or "doesn't feel good about gurus," or reasons over or resents the intrusion of a guide or mentor, is practicing a variety of me-yoga that may be empowering in the short term, but dangerous in the long.

A good guide, a knowledgeable companion, a spiritual friend or counselor who can keep us true to the main road, even as we take useful and intentional side trips, is worth his or her weight in gold. And more so now, when the number of neon arrows pointing to seductive detours increases exponentially year by year. Along the same lines, a vigilant and caring witness is an incomparable tool; one that, like a sharp ax, strikes at the roots of great loneliness, ennui or a profound sense of alienation. We all need one or more such witnesses, who by their presence and their attentive listening can affirm that our life matters. One who can hear our concerns, our worries, our fantasies, and not turn away. A witness who will meet our eyes, allowing us to *feel* that, in fact, we exist. A witness who will talk to us kindly and firmly, as the case may be, especially when we have spiraled into the habitual self-talk of loathing and recrimination.

The ultimate job of the witness is to serve as an external point of reference as we walk this highway of the heart—or highway of consciousness, if you prefer. This witness, this "other," is there to allow us to reconnect with our own heart's wisdom—vigilance, caring, discrimination, distinction-making, patience, humor ... the list goes on and on. Until such time as we have *realized* (not just intellectually, but in every cell of the body) the "ultimate witness"—some call this God, Truth, Compassion—and experienced that we are not and never have been separate from that, we will continue to suffer from loneliness, confusion and alienation. We will continue to need, passionately, and rightly so, the witness of the friend, the teacher, the guru, the counselor, the wise elder.

There is no shame in needing a witness. It is not the lesser or inferior choice. In fact, to try to be a lone warrior on this highway, or to initiate what author Kathleen Norris described as the "religion of one," is generally a much lonelier, more difficult choice and possibly dangerous choice. And besides, a witness who will take the wheel for a while, or sit at the campfire with us at night helping to keep the fire stoked, makes for a much easier trip, and a partial night's sleep.

I have such a witness in my husband Jere, who refuses to indulge my arguments for my limitations. "What's the bottom line, Regina?" he asks again and again, when I've temporarily forgotten who I am, and forgotten in what love I abide. His reminders are generally infuriating, in the moment. Something old and crystallized within me wants to stay small and powerless, victimized by circumstances, and asleep. Years and years of habitual self-forgetting have become so familiar that I immediately resent being deprived of this badge I hold onto as if it sums up my identity.

My friend Betsy has her stellar witness in the spiritual friendship she maintains with Abba Jonathan of God, a monk who occupies a hermitage in the Arizona desert. Betsy and I consider ourselves fortunate beyond words. It is no small gift to have found, or been found by, such a friend. And it takes work for me to nurture this aspect of my relationship with my husband. It is so easy to fall into the expected, the familiar, the easy, especially as we have lived together for over thirty years. It takes a lot of effort for Betsy to make time for her relationship with Abba Jonathan, especially as she lives in Idaho and he lives in the south of Arizona.

Rumi said that there are a thousand ways to kneel and kiss the ground. Left to our own devices, and encouraged by the experiences of our friends and witnesses, we might easily come up with a dozen or more ways to do this in our lifetime. Maybe even fifty! But a *thousand?* A thousand ways means that life has been fully transformed and that everything is sacred. A thousand ways means that prayer and praise is our only occupation.

One who can instruct us in "the thousand ways" by the radiance of his or her life is more than a companion. Such a one is a lighthouse—a spiritual master, guru or authentic teacher. Such a one has explored and lived the thousand ways; he or she sees and can point out, or help us clear away, the shards that would make kneeling in this spot sheer agony. The genuine guru or teacher has loved deeply, and thus reveals hundreds of moods and gestures of love.

My guru has allowed me to fall in love with him, and in that love my inner life has flourished. My relationship with him, far from being one of childish dependency (even though, Lord knows, I've tried repeatedly to burden him with this) has been a fierce demand to keep my eyes open and my head clear. He's warned me about my proximity to cliff edges, and shocked me to attention with a slap (figuratively speaking) when I've neglected to "put on my goggles" against "snow blindness." He's also danced with me, sung for me, invited me to travel with him into "dens of iniquity," gorgeous cathedrals and galleries of new art forms that I would never have explored on my own, given my stiff provincial history. He's requested that I undertake various projects that I never imagined I could do. He has been a constant *Yes* to the force of Divine love, and in and with him I've echoed that yes. He has never forgotten that I am not separate from the One, even though I've argued with him and fought to defend my limitations. All hail the gift of God that such a One can be in life!

Maybe you too have a guru or teacher or mentor in this inner life journey. If you do, I urge you to listen to him or her. Stay the course with them. When it is time to move on—to another teacher, or to another tradition, or to set up your own teaching life—you will be burnt to ash and blown there. You will *be* surrendered. In the meantime, recognize that you lose nothing in working with a real teacher as long as you are passionately listening within, and passionately self observing.

If you do *not* have a teacher, don't feel ready for a teacher, or simply haven't thought about needing one, ask yourself now if some guidance, clarity and companionship on this path might be welcome. If the answer is yes, sharpen your intention, wait patiently, read, and talk to someone whose judgment and clarity you trust about this issue.

If you *don't* want one, examine your reticence and pray for guidance to what the future may hold for you. Try to never say "never" about anything. If you *do* want a teacher, but haven't found *the* one, make a cry to heaven for this intention and wait patiently. Dig as deeply as possible into the writings and teachings of whatever faith tradition has the greatest resonance for you. Avoid trying to find the "best" teacher. There is none. There is only the best teacher for you!

There is so much joy in having companions in this way, and in walking the inner highway under the direction of one who has walked it before. Certainly there are risks; there are betraying friends and unscrupulous teachers. But, you're bright. Wake up! Abuse is abuse; but a challenge to ego is also a painful sting. Besides the great joy and comfort of having friends and guides, that sting is also what you develop sangha for; and why you come to the teacher. Why try to stay safe, anyway, unless you're so blissfully happy all the time that you don't want to change a thing. But, who among us can honestly say we know God? Who among us can honestly say he or she knows themselves? This is the blessing of the guide.

3. Discouragement and Dryness

Mother Teresa was plagued with discouragement and dryness throughout her dedicated life. If the devastating letters she confided to her spiritual mentors are to be believed, she suffered enormously, as much from the sense of having been abandoned by God, as from the tireless and self-effacing efforts that she made on behalf of others.[6]

Feeling abandoned, even Mother Teresa evidenced a ground of expectation that many of us cling to on this path. We expect that our efforts will have certain good results; "good" according to our own definitions. We all suffer, therefore, when we await what should be rather than accepting the simplicity of *what is*. Of course, when one has been gifted for years with great spiritual consolation, or with kundalini opening, or with mystical vision, understandably one would prefer that it last. To be blown into the devouring mouth of the volcano when one has labored for years to set up a peaceful camp on the mountain's peak would be seriously disorienting.

Spiritual dryness is talked about a lot in the Christian mystical tradition, and offered as a sign that the process of purification is well under way. After all, one must be cleansed from all attachments, especially the spiritual attachments, if one is to face the naked Real. In Buddhist and other non-theistic traditions, however, one isn't looking for signs from God. Instead, one ideally is welcoming the boredom, the ennui, the confusion, as grist for the mill. We learn about our grasping, we learn about our attachments, only by suffering them. We have to see what we are up to, and for many of us that takes a long, long time.

The joy of our inner life journey cannot be based upon some reward system—bliss experiences within, or the wise nods of approval from those who come to us for guidance. The delight of the inner life will only be found in the raw suchness of life as it is. To pray in silence is delight whether one is distracted or on fire with love *if* one is aware that praying is a miracle of communion between the human and the divine. Praying in silence is delight if prayer proceeds from awareness of one's being-presence—I am alive, here and now, on the spot. Any spiritual practice is delight and miracle when one is attuned to the unadorned wonder of breath arising, breath subsiding. Expecting an angelic message more important than the conversion of oxygen into CO_2 is a serious slap in the face of Divine generosity. Breathing is a miracle. To sit upright is a miracle. To hear a sound nearby, or far away, is a miracle. To be blessed with a fragrance of fried potatoes or Stargazer lilies is a miracle.

Even the pros—the yogis, the monks, the hermits, the Mother Teresas—have doubts, dry-spells and discouragement. Those for whom the spiritual journey is the day's primary job still go through periods when they wonder if all of this is really "doing any good" or "going anyplace." One cannot quantify the energetic of love. One cannot prove that one's heart on fire in Cleveland is in fact making any difference to the family in Croatia. And, isn't it a good thing? Otherwise, you can be sure that some bright marketing firm would have devised some system for making money on it.

To allow the mind a dominant voice in any discussion of the inner life is actually very dangerous, and especially when the devotionally-dry spells are the order of the day, as they often will be throughout our lives. What must be trusted above logic is that urgency toward an inner life, or a life of prayer and praise, that caused you to open this book. What must be relied upon is the desire for the communion with God, or deep adherence in Truth, that you knew, maybe long ago, was the outpouring of the well of silence. What can be trusted is the body's longing to offer itself for others, to heal pain, to touch a heart. The urgency of the buddha is the urgency to relieve suffering wherever it is found. That is real, and it cannot be measured, but it can be trusted.

Mind, however, wants constant reassurance in a domain that the inner life doesn't inhabit. Mind counts things. It keeps score. It makes points. Mind wants to be sure that it isn't wasting its time. Well, fine and good. That function of mind will always be present. Problem comes if we allow this judging function of good and bad, positive versus negative, to have power and authority for us where our longing for God or Truth or self-alignment is concerned. Giving such authority to mind is a very dangerous practice. It will keep one in hell.

The other day I passed a bus stop in the town where I live. On the back of the bench is some advertising space which is generally taken by a local group that tries to foster critical thinking. The American Society of Agnostics, or something. I generally find the clever sayings that appear there to be quite intriguing. But on this day I could only smile at what I judged to be a rather pathetic sentiment: "My church is my own mind," the bench ad read, credited to some statesman or other. A shiver ran through me. "What a sad church that must be," I thought. Anyone who has done even a modicum of self observation knows the chaos that reigns in the mind, and the way in which such chaos influences emotions; unless, of course, one has trained the mind to suppress *all* arising of feeling. In which case one has successfully cut themselves off from the life force.

Oh well, let's give this old dead white guy (probably) who wrote the quote the benefit of the doubt. Let's imagine that he is a bodhisattva who has pierced the nature of mind and now lives spontaneously happy in the domain of accepting just what is, in every moment. This is where our being-presence and attention to the inner life will take us—to the spontaneous joy and the natural outpouring of service. Yet, as long as we're counting, expecting and doubting we're discouraging ourselves.

Write out the truth for yourself and post it somewhere to view it frequently: "One day, long ago, I knew beyond doubt that Love was real. I will remain unshaken in that, regardless of the distractions of mind. I will weather this storm."

And then pray some more: "Oh, God help me to weather this storm that would blow me from you. Oh, let me simply be with *what is* rather than needing the mind's approval."

The Noonday Devil

My husband Jere was reading Kathleen Norris's new book, *Acedia & me*, as I wrote this chapter.[7] Acedia in the dictionary is often defined as "apathy," "boredom," or "torpor." But, as Norris explains, these words hardly do it justice. She takes us to the roots of this word, quoting in the frontmatter of her book the fourth century monk Evagrius Ponticus, the author of *The Praktikos*, who wrote to other desert hermits and monatics: "The demon of *acedia*—also called the noonday demon—is the one that causes the most serious trouble of all." As we consider dryness and discouragement in the inner life we are in fact defining acedia, the noonday devil so well known to the monk in the solitude of a desert hermitage: "I'm tired of this, let's get on to other things," or "What's the use?" or "Why bother?"

Yes, we all know acedia in our own ways and forms. This slump that occurs when one has nothing to look forward to except more of the same, especially since the current "same" is extraordinarily without interest. Full on boredom, tedium, lack of energy to move at all, no less to move forward—this is life as it sometimes is. And, this is a big pitfall in any life, even in one that would include self observation, prayer, spiritual practice. Norris quotes Evagrius further saying, that once this acedia-devil is confronted and transformed, no other demons follow. This is obviously the big one. When this one is defeated "... only a state of deep peace and indescribable joy arise out of the struggle."

Of course this argument makes perfectly logical sense to us when we stand on a platform supported by distractions. Sure, we say, I agree! Once there is nothing to look forward to, and one has fully embraced *just this*, without trying to get out, the peace of the awesome present moment creates indescribable joy. But, attempt to drop some of these distractions and see what happens.

Undertaking an extended retreat one encounters the noonday devil as early as the second day. We've geared ourselves up for the occasion and arranged our lives well. We've packed our bags and lined up all sorts of expectations, whether consciously or not, about how great or how necessary this retreat is going to be. But, when one is actually settled in—when the statues have been placed and the rugs adjusted—one stares at the meditation cushion and says, "Is that all there is?"

And, if one is able to be honest, the answer is a resounding Yes. That *is* all there is. That *is* the place of emptiness, not knowing, not doing, waiting, listening, observation without movement, and not much more. In fact, nothing more.

The temptation is always to create something out of nothing. This is in fact the essence of the creative process. The empty place of waiting gets so easily translated into some mysterious expectation of a visitation from the

Divine. The "not knowing" becomes a silent attachment to satori, if not for full-on enlightenment. The "not doing" becomes a form of discipline which earns points for the one who expects to be hailed as a warrior based on one's endurance; and the list of subtle expectations (and not so subtle intentions) begins to grow longer and longer.

Ah, and herein we are helpless. How can we do otherwise? And that seems to be the point. We can't!

The whole purpose of attending to the inner life is not about becoming a better anything ... or an enlightened nothing. The point is to shine a precise laser of light on the many varieties of illusion—be it pride or acedia—and to simply let them (these illusions) do whatever it is that phantoms do when exposed to a light.

How we want to fix it! Whatever *it* is. But, as my guides have instructed me, and as I will recommend to you, "fixing" may be the worst possible strategy. Fixing brings in all kinds of practices, attitudes and tools that in many cases will simply muck up and delay the works. Like when my computer apparently freezes up and I immediately call Technical Support. Often, before I know it, I've got some well-meaning eighteen-year-old techie telling me how I have to buy a new backup device to copy my hard drive to, and selling me a new $300 program.

Or, perhaps a better example: when my grandchild starts to cry and, instead of sitting calmly until I can understand her need, I start a huge song and dance to distract her from her pain. Such theatrics generally take much more energy than the situation calls for, and soon agitate me. I can end up making everything worse, to the point of total meltdown, for both of us.

"If it isn't broken, don't fix it" is surely sage advice. How deeply this fear runs—the fear that we are somehow broken. It is a fact of life that everything in nature has cracks or creases in it—human bodies, rock cliffs ascending to 14,000 feet, the centers of a dahlia blossom. To face boredom, tedium and/or meaningless and empty prayer is either a chance for dehumanizing pain, when not viewed consciously, or a chance for profound rest and utter peace. Nothing is nothing, and those who have lived within it tell us it is suffused with compassion.

Nothing lasts, neither boredom nor bliss. We don't stay awake or stay conscious permanently, until we *are that*, and even then "enlightenment is the knowledge that all things are transitory, including enlightenment," my spiritual master cautions. Or, as he has said elsewhere, the moment of transformation is "not our business." Rather, our business is to practice *now*. Our business is to keep coming back, coming home to the body, renewing intention, relaxing into what is, watching the mind's wild antics and not identifying with them. Our business is to remember, once again, where and how and who we are, to see what we are doing, and to drop it all and move on. This business of practicing with tedium and terror and exultation, all of it—the work of coming home—is synonymous with igniting the inner life.

4. Middle-Aged Stodginess

The tendency to get someplace, even some remarkable inner place, and coast toward home from there is part of the normal pattern of inertia or negative entropy that growing older entails. It's normal for bodies at rest to stay at rest. It's normal to slow the pace as your knees get creaky. But I'm not speaking about the physical domain here. It's more the attitude of "been there, done that" about the inner life that I'm referring to.

I've seen long-term spiritual practitioners who appear to have settled in, hunkered down to enjoy their retirement. They speak softly and even wisely when asked a question, but their life force is very thin. Ask them to join you for a new challenge—like a three-day juice fast, or to read some new book about the sacred art of tatouage, no less invite them to accompany you to India, or even to a weekend *sesshin* at a zendo—and you're liable to get a long story and a look of surprise. My teacher calls the condition "middle-aged stodginess," and he testifies to the fact that it can affect our work life, our family life and most seriously, our inner life.

"I'm too old for that" is a big and very powerful excuse. Although it often comes in handy, like when you take your grandchildren to Disneyland and they want you to accompany them on some terrifying ride. But unfortunately it gets used to cover everything from outright terror to mild discomfort. We use it to deny ourselves experiences that we are afraid we may fail at, in the same way that a ten-year-old kid says, "I don't like soccer." When we turn aside from the next risk based on middle-aged stodginess (and some people in their twenties are infected), be that risk minute or gigantic, we may miss a serious opportunity to warm up our inner life. It takes courage to explore the inner life. It takes courage to really see what we're up to and to "sit with" some discomfort until we gain some clarity about what is really bothering us.

I'm not talking about denial of the natural process and grace of aging or maturing. Nor am I advocating the typical "let's be young at heart" school of advertising. Looking in the wellness-oriented lifestyle magazines you get this message all the time: "Don't sit down and be satisfied. Get out there and be young again, even if only young at heart." The difference here is one of context. These "forever young" orientations of the current mind are all based in a fear of death—they encourage us to either deny it, or milk life for all it's worth while we still can. Correspondingly, these are the attitudes of ego maintenance. Keeping the ego—the "I like/I don't like"; the "it's all about me," or "what about *me*?" and the "mine, mine, mine, mine"—in charge of the show for as long as possible is the status quo of the cultural milieu. It is walking while asleep; unaware life; life unexamined. It is living death.

The attitude of risk-taking that I am referring to is one that puts ego on the cutting board just as the chef starts chopping the salad. One takes the risk with the hope (although it generally feels more like dread) of getting used for the meal. My guru is just such a master chef and he wields a powerful knife. The goddess Kali and numerous other Hindu deities hold a sword for this same purpose. The Divine as Mother has an urgency that her children come to the full realization of their true nature, pruned of all that prevents their full flowering. Christ impaled on the cross exemplifies this fierce grace of transformation.

At sixty-six and challenged with cancer, my teacher/ guru still toured Europe with his two performance bands. Their schedule was grueling. They drove from Barcelona to Frankfurt through the night, and then performed, packed up, and headed off to northern France to catch the ferry to London. He sings, he writes hundreds of songs, and he serves as the quiet center of the hurricane of the forty or more roadies, students, associates and friends who traipse along for the fun of the tour. Onstage, he whips the musicians into a frenzy, to the delight of their audiences. Offstage, he demands (and sometimes has to beg for) a rigorous attention to detail, to maintenance of practice, to self-sacrifice, to kindness, generosity and compassion, no matter what the hour and how little sleep one has gotten the night before. He chops off our ego-enthralled heads with bitter sarcasm, and cuts into our hearts with his tender attention to everyone's children. Being a member of his band is an invitation to exhaustion, to exposing one's rough edges in the presence of others (you simply can't keep it together under such stress for more than a few days!), and to exuberance. Life force pours from him, and he seems to know exactly where to poke to get it flowing in his companions.

The intention of his work with music is for others—–for those in the bands, as well as for his audiences. But, if asked to choose only one, he would say without hesitation that it is *all* for those of us who work with him, whether we're on the tour or answering the phones back home in the office. When we choose to play his game or accompany his lila, we are taking a risk that belies middle-aged stodginess and casts our vote for annihilation in love. For those with the courage to ride along, the exhaustion and chaos of the band tour is all about igniting the inner life.

5. Erotic Fantasies

Some people confuse this conversation about the inner life with a fantasy-filled existence. Their inner worlds are populated by gorgeous men or women who suddenly discover them, solve all their financial worries, and then take them to bed. I certainly don't imagine that *you*, dear reader, are one of those. However, I do know that the literature of mystical union is often highly erotic—from the *Song of Songs*, to the Ras Lila about the love play of Lord Krishna, to the passionate intimacy of Rumi's poetry. And I do know that the body is part and parcel of the mix when the inner life is undergoing transformation. The forces that open the third eye or the first chakra at the base of the spine are opened by kundalini (serpent power) energy, and are therefore strong and erotic. These energies awaken the body from a type of sleep. Mistakenly, however, such energies can kindle notions of cosmic sex. Seriously, I have seen advertisements for books or workshops that teach you how to make mind-blowing love with an angel, or some visiting "Beloved." I've read a book recently, written by a well-known Hollywood movie actress, in which she made a 500-mile pilgrimage in northern Spain—a journey meant to dismember the ego. Yet this woman was fiercely engaged in her fantasies of angelic visitations and cosmic sex with a saintly messenger of days gone by. Such "love" is cheap. Cheapened not by its orientation to pleasure—I'm all for pleasure, delight, joy! Rather it is cheapened because it is oriented to egoic aggrandizement, as in "Hey, look over here. *I'm* making love with an angel, *for God's sake!*"

Our fantasies, sexual or otherwise, build the walls of our prisons. In the solitude of contemplative practice I can drift away into prayerful fantasies—visions, angelic messages, imagined conversations, brilliant lectures being delivered to admiring audiences. Unless we can really *see* that even our prayer life is motivated and nurtured by the need for affirmation and security, as mine often is, we cannot tell the truth about ourselves, and our inner work will never get off the ground. With fantasies we decorate our prison cells or our monastic cells with murals of the sky and the desert island, and we then proceed to live within the fantasy, temporarily forgetting that we are in prison. We miss life as it is.

A variation on fantasy is the conscious, purposeful use of visualization. A vast body of literature exists, particularly in the Buddhist Tantric tradition, in which the practitioner is instructed in visualizations that unite her with the deity. This literature is often highly detailed and consequently erotic, sometimes involving the penetration of the yoni with the lingam, and a posture that includes naked contact, male with female. The literature as well as the visualization practice naturally arouses sexual energy, and so the visualizer is challenged with ages-old dichotomies about the sexual and spiritual; the lower nature and the higher nature; what is sin and what is prayer! The practitioner is thus entering into territory that would be completely off limits to any righteous fundamentalist. And yet, paradoxically, the practitioner is doing this practice as a powerful means of annihilating all personal attachments.

Sexual energy *is* life energy. It will enter into the equation as we talk about igniting the inner life. Getting lost in the labyrinth of an erotic inner fantasy life is a guarantee that you will be late for the real meal, however, and miss the real deal. Handling sexual energy with joy and attention, consciously, rather than being run by it mechanically, is one of the surest ways of aligning with the creative and transformational power—the life force.

6. Attachments to the Senses, Materiality and Mortality

Have you ever wondered why apparently smart saints used austerities (sometimes extremely rigorous) to fuel their inner fire? This subject of self-denial (as the topic used to be called) or *tapas* (a Sanskrit word with the same meaning), or even the word "sacrifice" are not particularly in vogue. For too long, I think, we've operated under an Old Testament paradigm that demanded "an eye for an eye and a tooth for a tooth." We learned that we would be damned for our sins, and that we must struggle to earn our birthright. It is no wonder that so many have rebelled against "doing penance." The overlays to this phrase and this practice are much too coded with shame, self-loathing, and judgment. And yet ...

My good friend Dave was traveling in Europe a few years ago. One day, as he went to town to do some errands, he realized that he would be late for another appointment if he stopped to get himself a cappuccino. He was faced with the choice between honoring his word and being on time, or satisfying his immediate desire. He stopped for the coffee. He was late for his appointment, with no real excuse, and inconvenienced several other people in the process. Within a short time the blatant nature of his own selfishness flabbergasted him. He had never seen it quite so clearly. The sense of self-betrayal, that feeling that he had violated his own integrity, hung on like a damp towel on a humid day. But what could he *do* about it? The situation was over. He could never return to that moment of choice again and do things differently.

Dave decided that he wanted to provide himself with a stronger memory peg for this incident. He decided that he would take on a task that held some challenge for him, something that would drive home for him the failed integrity of his choice. He decided to forego dinner that night and let his grasping hunger be a reminding factor to him, for a few hours at least, that unless he worked with postponing gratification he would forever be victimized by his sense desires. He ate no dinner and went to bed uncomfortably hungry, but awake to his desire to build his self-control and self-respect.

117

Dave's "sacrifice" could have been viewed as a form of self punishment: I did something bad and now I will punish myself. But, knowing him, and hearing him describe the situation I knew that it was far from that limited context. Dave was exercising a conscious choice to reinforce his intention to develop conscience. He saw that the integrity of his inner life demanded it. I will never forget his story and the lesson it taught me.

My teacher, my guru, lives a life of simple and often invisible self-denial. He is never morbid about his *tapas*. Much the opposite, those who observe him from a distance would probably describe him as a man with enormous joie de vivre. For years he celebrated with us over elegant dinner parties; he traveled the continent of Europe with his bands and spent untold hours in cafes of every type, urging us to order the most decadent pastries on the menu. "Good for you!" he might exclaim when a chocolate mousse arrived at the table for one of his usually abstemious students. Yet, for those who have lived and worked around him for many years, Lee's self-mastery with regard to food, drink, sleep and the use of resources is obvious and extraordinary. His lunch meal typically consisted of a single apple, or a few fresh stalks of celery. Traveling, he would stop for meals essentially because the children in our company were becoming hungry and fussy, not because he chose to entertain or distract himself with food.

Does anybody deny themselves food today, unless they are on a diet motivated by the desire to look slim or feel healthier; or motivated by a diagnosis of a serious health condition? Does anybody deny themselves sleep for the purposes of working on themselves to overcome the attachment to comfort? Does anybody deny themselves material possessions for the simple reason that such denial can build "being"—a sense of integrity, an ability to be in the midst of great temptation and yet be undistracted?

Food is good. It can and should be celebrated. Beautiful things can lead us to remember the Beloved. Comfort may enhance a sense of restfulness, as we fall back into the arms of God. And yet, our need for comfort, convenience and immediate gratification can also be a serious detour on the inner highway. If, as is the case today, we come to demand and expect comfort; if, as is the case today, we cannot let the smallest blip of hunger arise without immediately seeking to satisfy it; if, as is the status quo, we are encouraged to accumulate so that we may keep up with what the "good life" demands, well, you do the math. What is the quality of an inner life that is only accessible when soft music is playing and incense is burning, and a glass of fine wine is within reach?

In the life of Kathryn Hulme, a writer and close student of George Gurdjieff, an example of self mastery stands out like a billboard on the road. Kathryn was a habitual smoker, and Gurdjieff pointed out that the smoking had become her master. When she protested that she was not enslaved, he called her bluff. On the spot, Kathryn snuffed out her cigarette in the ashtray in front of her and committed to abstain from smoking. The sacrifice of cigarettes was not an easy one for her, either internally or externally. But Gurdjieff instructed her and the group of women he worked with at the time that the suffering of such a decision was a means of building inner being. He suggested that they use a statement of intention, which was similar to a form of prayer, each time the desire to smoke arose: "I wish the result of this, my suffering, be my own, for Being."[8]

In Buddhism, similar practices encourage the offering of our discomfort as a means of accumulating "merit" that may be applied to relieve the sufferings of others. From my own roots in Catholicism, I can deeply appreciate that "giving up something for Lent" was based in a similar paradigm—one of self-mastery and remembrance. With our slight inconvenience we remembered the passion and death of Christ, and we also established within ourselves a strengthened means to resist grasping after every little treat in the pantry.

I'll have more to say on the subject of grasping and attachment in Chapter 8. For the time being, however, to take attachment and grasping after the good life a step further, let's take it to the moment of death. Let's imagine ourselves hooked up to a breathing tube, with the wild mind racing out of the control. Let's feel the attachment to family, friends, food and all things familiar. Ah, what then? Wouldn't you like to have a backlog of internal energy built by a life of self-control; a backlog of "being" built by the conscious use of all the tiny moment-to-moment desires that were consciously transformed, ready to rise to the occasion? I'm giving myself shivers as I write these words. I know *I* would!

7. Being a Good Soldier

So there I was on retreat, diligently walking in a circle inside my small round yurt, in the desert, in the middle of winter, with a storm blowing outside that caused the canvas walls to flab loudly. I was using my prayer beads, saying my mantra. What a trouper! The thought flashed across my mind that I was like a soldier marching, and that instead of a gun on my shoulder I had a rosary in my hand. Gun or rosary, the mood of the soldier—an intensely masculine energy—was predominant. The next thought that followed, without any conscious help from me, was that the Beloved, whatever form God's love might take, was reclining on my narrow bed, simply waiting for me to finish my drill and put down my weapon long enough for us to talk, or touch or gaze into each other's eyes.

The Beloved's patience struck me as seemingly endless. He or she will apparently wait forever, if necessary. Meanwhile, I was growing older, my hair was getting thinner, and I was slowly losing the opportunities for unknown possibility that this moment offered.

The diligent approach to practice is a valuable one to cultivate. It may be the urgency we need to get us to the meditation cushion every morning. Yet, it is not the only approach to practice, and certainly not the only context for igniting the inner life. Truth is, we need both—the masculine and the feminine; the Martha and the Mary; the form and the emptiness; the diligence and the melting into love. An approach based solely on rigid rules is *not* the way to cultivate the inner life. "Lighten up! Relax, will you," my teacher is constantly instructing. To ignite the inner life is not about doing it right or doing it one-hundred-percent of the time. Discipline and checklists may work in the army, but in sex or in the chamber of the heart they may crush the spontaneity of love.

When my adopted grandson was young, he would regularly sit in my lap. Most of the time he would lean forward to occupy himself with a small toy that he carried around, or to reach for my feet, or to examine his own amazing fingers. Periodically, however, he would remember that he was in my lap. With that, he would drop back, leaning into my body, turn his face up, look me in the eyes and say "Nana" with complete innocence and adoration. It was the purest acknowledgement I had ever received.

This same relaxation, this same falling back into the arms of the Divine, is an orientation that will strongly enhance our ability to ignite the inner life. It is not about lessening discipline but about increasing trust. When I was called upon to write an extensive biography of Yogi Ramsuratkumar, my teacher's guru, I was challenged beyond what I thought possible. Relaxation was not a mood that generally characterized my approach to the book. And yet, I learned more about true relaxation from doing that project than from any program of stress-reduction or any series of yogic breathing exercises. I learned that there were larger arms into which I could fall. Yes! The biography of this great saint was written because I rested in him, and let him direct the process. He did.

> "You can never fall from my lap."
> —Jellalamudhi Ma[9]

Such a relaxation doesn't only happen when the subject of one's project is a *mahasiddha* (a Master Awakener). It happens when the task at hand is a major housecleaning or an editorial job for a book of medical research. It happens when we realize that we are outwardly motivated instead of inwardly guided, and when we decide to do something about it, like "igniting the inner life." There *is* a Great Mother or a Divine Beloved or a Tao in which we can rest; on whom we can rely. Not because, like some magical giant who lives in the high mountains, this One comes down to visit us, but because (whether we *feel* it or not) we are not separate from that One. From the perspective of the Mother's lap or the universe's heart, the detours in the road are seen long before we are on top of them. From that perspective, the reality of love is seen for what it is, everything!

> [T]here is something mysterious at the heart of things, something we can't figure out or get control of. It's a mighty big ocean whose surface we skim. If we lean back into that experience, we're more and more at peace with what isn't certain, and less and less in a chronic state of complaint at what W.H. Auden called the disobedience of the daydream. We spend so much time disappointed in life for being life. But as we feel less and less resistance to things as they are, as peace grows in the midst of uncertainty, kindness is not far behind. We're not at war with life so much anymore, and that is a kinder way to be. When we're not fighting with life, or turning away from it, joining in seems to come pretty naturally. Someone is hungry; it's time to make dinner. An election turns out badly; where do we go from here?   —Joan Sutherland[10]

As we proceed together here I will remind you again and again to relax, as my beloved teacher constantly reminds me. A poem he wrote to his master, Yogi Ramsuratkumar, one which I particularly cherish, contains these lines:

> … What to do, what to do, oh Light?
>   Persist, dig deeper, try harder
> and above all, relax, and let you do Your Work
>   on us and in us, above, below, beyond
> and around us, to let you have Your Way
>   to allow our hearts to melt with love,

> and more crucially, to allow our crystallized
> mechanicality to soften and meld, to meld
> itself to Your Instruction and Your Word ...[11]

Lee obviously wrote this for all who would seriously undertake to practice a way of surrender. He was speaking of the need for vigilance, for efforts, for the willingness to look at the root of ego's motivations. Yet his overall message was that we all needed to relax. Reading this poem on retreat, with the benefit of nothing else to do, I saw the unbelievably rigid control mechanisms (that "crystallized mechanicality") that dominate my daily life. I am not speaking of control in the sense of fine tuning my practice, but control in the sense of trying to organize, plan, cover all the bases, keep things safe, make it all turn out nice. Control, as I generally practice it, is the opposite of relaxation. I saw that this control is not limited to my work, or the way in which I plan a trip. My inner life is under such tight control most of the time that it takes the shock of a retreat to alert me to the stranglehold in which I am holding myself, my guru and God. My hands are often grasping a siphon, carefully cutting off how much grace I allow myself to take. When I realize this, my sojourn in the desert is immediately transformed from a test of endurance to an exercise in letting go.

The muscles of the exterior of the body know how to tense and relax. But the relaxation that comes from an inner "falling into God" is of an entirely distinct nature. These muscles are not easily touched, even by the deepest form of massage. They are the muscles around the heart and around the core of the vital center—the muscles of the inner body. It seems that only with *help* can these be attended to. On retreat I came to understand that the blessing of God's love can release these muscles by making Its presence known more dynamically within the cells. When I am willing to take the time to practice—immersing myself in attention, prayer, inner listening, reading from sources of teaching, through all the means left at my disposal—that presence in the cells is enlivened to the point where it cannot be denied. It throbs. The man or woman who feels this must then simply say YES, again and again and again.

During a trip to Mexico City in 2004, Lee spoke to the sangha and assembled friends there about this need to relax. Here again he wasn't speaking of taking a vacation. Rather, he was reminding his guests that our normal condition is one of resistance to *what is*; our normal stance is one of defense against the truth of *Only God*; our modus operandi is denial of our true nature, which is one of union with the Divine. When, with deeply furrowed brows, we ask questions of our guides or gurus that reflect our assumption of separation, or make comments that proclaim life as a problem, or speak in a way that exaggerates and advertises our self-hating condition, or that puts the master on some unreachable cloud and puts us in the mud, we are tensed and unhappy, and we are betraying the trust in the Divine that our teachers are attempting to remind us of.

When Lee tells me to relax, or makes a joke to me, he is not being silly or cute. He is honestly attempting to help me to loosen this death-like grip with which I hold onto my illusions. Often, I stubbornly refuse to take his suggestions to relax seriously. I think he is just being a nice guy, but he isn't. He is speaking the deepest truth and offering me the most significant help he can offer. If he laughs—with me, or at me, or at nothing at all—like his Father, Yogi Ramsuratkumar, Lee is urgently reminding me and others that we have nothing to worry about; that "Father in heaven" is everywhere, in everything, past, present, future; and that we can never ever be separated from that.

This relaxing into trust might just be the primary practice to assure us a good life, an ardent inner life and a good death. We have no idea what our last weeks or months or days or hours will be like. Yet, if we have been practicing this type of relaxation—letting love have love's way with us—what more will we need to do?

8. Staying in Charge

Donald was dying. The husband of a good friend, Donald learned in August that he had a virulent form of cancer due to his exposure to Agent Orange during the Vietnam War, in which he had served on the front lines as a medic. He was dead in late December.

In early December, before I left town for three weeks, I paid him a visit and we embraced for what I assumed would be the last time. I promised to pray for him during my time away. One morning during the next week, as I sat quietly in meditation, I thought strongly of Donald and wondered if that meant he had passed on. But since I rarely trust such psychic impressions, I instead wrote him a letter expressing my love and caring once again, and sent it off to him.

The morning that I returned home there was an urgent message waiting for me. "Please come to visit Donald," it said, "he is asking for you." What a gift, I thought to myself. This call had immediately eschewed any idea I may have held about how I needed a gentle transition from my restful weeks away to the demanding schedules of my workaday world. It was, therefore, the first test of the usefulness of my time apart: Would I say yes and move into the demand seamlessly, or not?

In half an hour I was on my way to Donald's home, covering the forty-five miles with ease and a joyful heart, but also nervous as to what his call might entail. He was noticeably weaker and significantly more emaciated than when I had left him twenty-one days ago. His voice was little more than a whisper. But his eyes were radiant and I suspected that he was already tasting the sweetness of letting go.

"Regina," he said, getting to the point with no wasted niceties, "I can't surrender to God. I don't know *how* to surrender to God." In a short sentence he told me that he had been diligently invoking the name of God in the person of Yogi Ramsuratkumar, the great beggar saint, but still he was at a loss for how to let go completely into that love.

"*You* can't surrender, Donald," I said authoritatively, as if I really knew what I was talking about, "but God *can surrender you.* All you need to do is to keep your focus and your intention. Make that your prayer: 'Surrender me to Thee.'" The teaching of that moment was unrehearsed, but certainly not original. Inwardly I thanked my spiritual teacher for these words.

Donald smiled when I spoke, and I could see that he was considering my direction with great attention. He was also very very tired, so I kissed him on his cheek and left the room.

That evening he lapsed into a coma, and the next night, just a little more than twenty-four hours later, Donald died with great peace.

Falling Off the Edge of the World

The assurance I was able to give Donald was the result of my teacher's grace, and it was intensified by an experience I had lived through during my time away prior to his death.

The subject of what it means to surrender to God has long been an issue I have pondered. Actually, the word "surrender" isn't one that adequately communicates what the true desire is, although it comes close. For me, desiring to surrender is a yearning for intimacy, without those NO TRESPASSING signs I use to desperately wall off pieces of "my" territory against intrusion from anyone or anything else, including Divine Love. Perhaps you know this yearning too—like when you're playing with a child; or out with a friend to whom you would like to open your heart; or spending a quiet evening with your lover. Only, for some reason, known or unknown, your move or theirs, the two of you can't seem to get any traction—in the play, or the opening up or the lovemaking. You're guarding something ... or they are. Who's to tell? But, for whatever reason, somebody's NO is bumping up against somebody-else's MAYBE.

Oh, I wouldn't readily admit this. But, when I get to the bottom line of my life I find that there are many many NO's still in operation. No's to being seen in all my wounded splendor. No's to receiving the unconditional love of God, or the sweet blessing of life just as it is. I'm resisting. And so, during this trip I practiced specifically saying YES to everything that arose—whether in the food I was served, the weather that greeted me each morning, or any thoughts of fear that tried to take possession of the mind at any unguarded moment. Saying YES is a powerful practice, as I learned the day I took a short walk that turned out to be a little detour that would recontexualize my life.

Walking along a hillside nearby the house in which I stayed, as I repeated a mantra and fingered my prayer beads, I was stopped in mid-step by an awareness that I was literally approaching the edge of the known universe. *My known universe!* There was no vision. There were no lights. There were certainly no voices of guidance or prophecy. But there was an interior *knowing* that surrender as I had always prayed for it was right there in front of me. I was on the edge of the abyss of myself, and about to step off into nothingness, if only I put my foot down to complete that awesome step. *Freeze!*

I know what it means now when people say that at the moment of death your whole life passes before you, because while I didn't replay my temporal drama, I did have full consciousness that all the roles, all the affectations, all the definitions of who this being called "Regina" was *now*, and had been for the last fifty-plus years, was poised there, ready to be sucked away into that great void under my right foot. Completing that step would mean that *everything* I had previously held to and used to recognize *who I was*, and what I thought I needed or wanted, would be fully undermined. That "self" would be obliterated as completely as a raging flood obliterates a house built on the river banks.

Time really did stand still in this experience, as images of this "Regina" personality and all the ways in which she so diligently tries to keep it together, and all the approval she seeks in keeping it that way, were so obvious. But more. Not only was this revelation about how "Regina" kept this personality in place; it was also about the expectations from everyone and everything in the environment that wanted "me" to remain just as predictable as ever. These specters too jumped up to confront me. Did I *really* want to surrender that much!? The question wasn't verbalized, but it was cognized. Was I ready for there to be *nothing* familiar—no secure harbors, perhaps even madness or chaos—on the other side? Was I ready to put my foot where my yearning was?

Before "I" could decide, the mid-air foot swung around to my right, and I stepped backward.

I'm Not in Charge

I returned to my room exhausted but also exhilarated. Whatever "that" was, clearly it contained a gift. But, exactly what that gift was I couldn't yet say. I knew I had been given a glimpse of something that I had prayed for. I had a visceral *knowing* of the pure spontaneity that might lie on the other side of defended grasping—my usual way of life. I had seen, for a split second, a territory in which mind is free, unencumbered by the programs that mechanically determine every response. And, I had said, quite definitively, "No thanks. Not now."

Hours later, in solitude, over my soup supper, I recognized that I still wasn't feeling bad about my stepping away. Luckily, and undoubtedly all connected to the grace that the whole experience had been, a big YES had intervened, which stayed with me still. YES, I said, to what might normally have been a source of regret or disappointment. YES, I said, even enthusiastically, to my failure to leap into the void. At the back of my mind, I was aware that the voices of self-judgment and deprecation were trying to make themselves heard. But, they were easily being drowned out in the chorus of YES that echoed around me.

Some supposed advancements are just not timely. Some miles in the direction of the holy mountain of our pure intention have got to be walked slowly and diligently. For many years, perhaps, we must stay on the main road, building balance and inner strength, before the shortcut is indicated. My time for surrender hadn't come, obviously, because "it"—meaning the leap, the act of surrender—had not been taken.

As the sun set, instead of being disappointed I was happy. That back step, I realized, was *not* a conscious one. Even if the mind had wanted to take the plunge, the rest of the psycho-physical complex generally known as "Regina" was not willing to follow through. "One cannot surrender oneself," my teacher had explained numerous times over the years, and I had heard him. But that night, as I arranged the curtains over my windows in preparation for the cold and wind of the December night, I *knew* that bit of teaching in a real way. I would "be surrendered"— but only when and if that surrender, that obliteration of the past and openness to God's will beyond everything that I had previously known, could be *lived* and used for the benefit of God's work. I would "be surrendered" only when "I" was ready to be taken out of the picture. In God's own good time.

And, in the meantime? My teacher's advice had always been, and still is: stay in place, don't reach, relax, focus intention and practice. My counsel to Donald came from knowing this.

This recognition—of just how "not in charge" the "I" is—is an invaluable contemplation on this spiritual journey.

Contemplating the "Not In Charge"

Everything I've learned about relaxing and surrendering contradicts what I thought it was years ago. Everything I've learned has been infused or awakened in me by the guru's grace, particularly through the unique circumstances of being blessed with a project that was incomprehensible to my rational mind; a project for which I felt completely inadequate and unworthy; a project that both stretched and stressed me to limits that hitherto I had only imagined. In asking me to write a biography of his beloved guru, Yogi Ramsuratkumar, Lee offered me a prize form of work stress. He left me in the hands of my subject, the blessed beggar of Tiruvannamalai, and that was the greatest gift of all.

Yogi Ramsuratkumar is a master in all respects. A little neurosis like my obsessive stress is nothing to him. As I worked on the book project, the greater my anxiety the more he was there to soothe it, assuring me again and again that it was *his* project, and if I would simply trust that, and trust him—trust how he was working *in* me *as* me, with all the skills and enthusiasms I had for research, for storytelling, for the willingness to put in the time, no matter what—he would accomplish his purpose through me.

The relaxation of my compulsive need to manage everything that Yogi Ramsuratkumar was instructing me in was a relaxation of cosmic proportions. He himself was a master of it—he was *always* Working; working so constantly that he didn't have time for a bath or a change of clothes, yet he still sat silently, he sat patiently, he danced in the temple or walked the mountain path as if there was nothing in the world that was more important to do, he dissolved into the emptiness of the heart of God. He was absorbed, all the time, by only God, and spent his days chanting the name of Ram and sharing coffee with his devotees. We would be hard-pressed to find one more useless than he was in the eyes of the world.

In proving his constancy to me, day in and day out, his constant availability in the writing of the book, Yogi Ramsuratkumar slowly slowly gained my trust. His trustworthiness began to loom larger than the voices of protest, the "I can't do this" voices; the "Lee will hate this" voices; the "the devotees will be embarrassed for me" voices; the "never good enough" and the "you blew it this time" songs that play incessantly, prompted by ego who has her finger glued to the replay button. Day by day his guidance grew in both subtlety and precision. Certainly it was Regina's experience as a writer and Regina's fingers on the computer, but it was him speaking from within; him allowing certain roads to dead-end quickly, and certain books or resources to apparently materialize from nowhere.

I came to learn in my common experience what writers have always known about the relationship with the Muse: that there is a price to be paid, by way of putting the body on the line, but when the Muse is smiling (and Yogi Ramsuratkumar is *always* smiling) there is wonder, joy, even ecstasy in the fulfillment of the task. On the days when the Muse (or some creative sense of inspiration) is seemingly absent, one must pay her (him) the homage anyway. One must remain vigilant even if the Muse sleeps.

Yogi Ramsuratkumar was and still is my Muse, in the most exalted sense of the term. He slowly let me in on the secret of how to relax, really *relax*, not some pseudo-relaxation choice to go to the movies. He slowly showed me how to take a tiny step back from the work in progress, or the conversation I was having. He taught me how to lean back (a few inches only were necessary) so that I was leaning back against him. He taught me that I was like a child seated on the mother's lap; even though I was still a child who was constantly distracted with my new toys. But, as far as he was concerned, apparently that was okay too. As soon as my fascination abated somewhat, or when I needed to rest a bit, he taught me how to fall back ever so slightly so that I was nestled in his arms, my head against his heart.

Yogi Ramsuratkumar was my Divine Mother throughout this period. I was actively writing a huge book, and yet I was *being* surrendered.

9. Sentimentalismo

Love. Ah, sweet love ... maybe even Divine Love. The spark, the voice of God? All so lovely and poetic sounding, and reminding me of a children's song: "There's a little wheel a turnin' in my heart ... In my haaaa-ah-art, in my haaaa-ah-art. There's a little wheel a turnin' ... [flame a burnin'?] ... in my heart."

Yes, most of us know this feeling and this experience— the feeling connected with puppies, and adorable babies saying amazing things, and Christmas trees all aglow. It is also evoked by the sight of the bloated belly of the African baby whose mother is dying of AIDS. It is the reason why such emotion-based campaigns for fundraising are so successful, especially over the holidays when our own tables are overflowing with delectable farm-raised beef and organic veggies. We are machines, triggered this way by one stimulus and that way by another. Guilt, yes, is a great way to get people to move their hands to their wallets.

And so we light our candles, and light our incense that reminds us of the last trip to India or the Benediction of the Blessed Sacrament, and maybe we put on a tape of Gregorian chant or maybe one of Japanese flute if we're more the world music type, and we settle down to have a romantic evening with God. And low and behold, surprise of all surprises, the heart starts warming up and pretty soon we are feeling the indications of that wave of bliss that carried us away the night before, or last week, or whenever.

Like the erotic fantasies mentioned earlier, romanticism, or *sentimentalismo* as my Spanish-speaking sisters call it so appropriately, is a great trap in the inner life. I'm sorry to have to burst that bubble, but that is hopefully why you are reading this book.

I know whereof I speak, being an extraordinarily sentimental type, and quite sensual to boot. I have great associations with the trappings of the heart chamber, which Katherine Mansfield described so exactly in her classic short story, *Bliss:* "—as though you'd suddenly swallowed a bright piece of that late afternoon sun and it burned in your bosom, sending out a little shower of sparks into every particle, into every finger and toe?"[12]

I must continually remind myself that the cultivation of the inner life is not for the purpose of generating more warm cuddlies. Ideally, we immerse ourselves in the inner life to be undone so that we might serve creation as a clear glass or a really strong vehicle able to be on fire with love in the most unsentimentally charged places, like the waiting room at the cancer-treatment center, or the airport on the day before Thanksgiving when a blizzard has closed down the runways. Or when we hear of the latest terrorist attack somewhere in the world. Can we keep the heart open in hell? And if so are we willing to stay there as long as possible, as Chögyam Trungpa Rinpoche said when asked what to do when you find yourself in hell.

Let's get down to specifics, as I assume you are reading this because you are serious about the inner life. First off, I'm not saying that romance and sentiment are bad or wrong. I'm simply suggesting that such emotional moods should not go unexamined, because they can be dangerous detours. This doesn't mean that they have to be analyzed. There is a really big difference between analyzing (especially if there is any tendency on your part for self-hatred), and simply noting that these elements are present as two factors in a big mix. The point is, we don't want to deny such bliss experiences, nor do we want to indulge them. Just that we *be with* what is present before we start signing up for some graduate level course in contemplation, or booking our ticket to Zaire to work for the needy there. Like everything under scrutiny of self observation, we notice and accept, with humble honesty about what we notice.

Second, recognize that heart-stirring emotionalism is a universal phenomenon. I'm sure that instigators of genocide had it for their own children. And the Chinese guards who killed thousands of Tibetan monks and nuns had it for their own mothers. If in fact what you feel *is* Divine love itself and not some variety of heartburn, such a new way of seeing or at least looking at the world will ultimately transform everything. It will destroy the old sentimentalismo and replace it with a real heart of gold, fierce with fire. A mature inner life is deep rooted. It is not blown apart by the winds of circumstance, by praise nor blame, by riches or poverty. Well, I think you get the picture.

Sentimentality can be an early form of spiritual absorption, so if you are new at this inner life practice don't discount it; that is, don't deny your emotions or attachments or judge them as bad or wrong. The external indicators that might be dismissed as superficial sentimentality might also be objective forms of ritual—the music of Mozart can be used in a wide variety of ways, subjectively or objectively. Such emotion-laden forms might be valuable assists in the deepening of one's inner life, it's all in how you relate to them.

On the other hand, dropping the forms, even temporarily, might also open new possibilities for inner work. For years and years my prayer life was sentimentally interwoven with the need for images, for the smell of a particular kind of incense, with a shrine full of lighted candles. Then, I started making solitary retreats in a desert hermitage in northern Arizona. The land there was so vulnerable to prairie fires that the retreat directors asked that no candles or incense be used, ever, in the wood frame huts or outdoors.

No candles?! No incense?! I was angry, actually, learning of this rule, even though I understood the reason for it. But the experience demanded that I examine my attachment to these forms and open myself to discover their real meaning, as well as my attachments—based in sentimentality—to them.

After several such retreats I can report that my relationship to light in general, and sunlight in particular, has changed dramatically since being without candles for three weeks at a time. I found a new relationship to the light of the moon and the starlight sky, without candles. I developed a series of new and personally meaningful rituals for welcoming the dawn and sunset, all because I was invited to by the circumstance of being without fire. Without incense that I could burn, I found pine sap and juniper berries to make fragrant offerings with. I used crushed sage and rubbed essential oils on my wrists and on the hands and feet of my bronze icons, my cross, my prayer beads.

Being without what I thought was essential to the creation of a certain mood of contemplation has actually allowed me to deepen and more greatly appreciate my relationships to fire and light and incense. It is so easy to take anything for granted. It is also true that new approaches may yield remarkable side benefits.

A few years ago I gave a seminar on spirituality for a group of about thirty Mexican women in Mexico City. Their expressions of gratitude and appreciation toward me were so effusive that I soon realized that they were focusing their attention on *me* rather than on their own magnificent and prayer-yearning hearts. The energy of praise that should have been brought to their altar in the inner chamber of being was being lavishly showered on me. Of course my ego might have loved this, were it not for the sword on a thread that my teacher has poised above my head. He has taught me that it doesn't take much to lose one's work—that is, to be taken in by distraction and spiritual pride—and fall into believing that the shovel (the instrument) is responsible for the temple (God's work).

I asked the women to give me a word to describe such effusive praise and they suggested "sentimentalismo." A great sounding word, and one that exactly described the sticky feeling of being showered with praise above and beyond the necessary acknowledgement of simple gratitude. "Yes," I declared on hearing it, "that would be the word to characterize this tendency, and would serve our work together as a reminding factor."

And so, throughout our time in this sacred seminar I invited the women to *feel* their gratitude but not to express it to me. Rather, to turn it *in*, to the inner altar. To the feet of the Beloved who lives "in you, as you," as Swami Muktananda instructed. They did this to the best of their ability, even though I heard their reports that it was a particularly challenging exercise. Essentially, the challenge was to go deeper with the energies of joy, appreciation, praise, gratitude, longing, love.

They also asked me what to do with these energies once they were internalized. I suggested that "doing something with" was not the issue, so much as letting themselves *feel* the energies; breathing into the energies; creating space in the heart to hold the energies; watching themselves to see or feel what happened with these energies when they were not expressed. I also recommended that they could place or dedicate the energies, much like one takes a gift or an offering to the altar and lays it down, representative of one's desire to offer oneself to God. I asked them to lay their energies, which were actually energy-prayers, on the heart's altar and ask—that is, intend—that these be used for the deepening of their own love, as well as for the benefit of others. And then to wait patiently, observing what if anything happened.

They did as I suggested. What happened is written in their hearts.

I am convinced beyond the shadow of a doubt that we will be *shown* how to next proceed when our intention is clearly to rout out what is sticky and make smooth the rough road that keeps us from the desire of our hearts.

The Healing Time

Finally on my way to yes
I bump into
all the places
where I said no
to my life
all the untended wounds
the red and purple scars
those hieroglyphs of pain
carved into my skin, my bones,
those coded messages
that send me down
the wrong street
again and again
where I find them
the old wounds
the old misdirections
and I lift them
one by one
close to my heart
and I say ... holy
    holy.

—Pesha Gertler[1]

Chapter 7

Pilgrimage and the Inner Life

India is filled with places of pilgrimage. Shrines, temples, holy mountains and rivers, these attract millions of visitors every year. Devout Indians will often pile the whole family into a train car or onto a bus, along with assorted baggage (sometimes with cookstove and bag of rice), and journey hundreds of miles to offer prayers of petition or gratitude to a favorite deity. They will think nothing of joining two million others who are congregating for a special religious holiday, like the holiday during which a bath in the now poisonously polluted Ganges River is thought to be a ticket to liberation.

Places of pilgrimage in India are known esoterically as *teertha*, a term meaning a crossroads or a doorway. The teertha is the place at which two worlds meet, and this is precisely why we make pilgrimages, to encounter access to this other world. Teertha, or pilgrimage sites, therefore, are places where magic and miracles can happen. In fact, such miracles are expected, as we hear in the testimonies of thousands who have made the pilgrimage to Lourdes.

The teertha, however, is not exclusively an external spot. These places of access, these pilgrimage destinations, can be within us as well. The seeker or the pilgrim can journey to the heart of himself or herself by any number of paths. Here, resting in the guesthouse of the heart, he or she may find access to the world in which love is the currency; the place in which the Presence of God is tangible.

This interior pilgrimage, to one's true heart, is the path offered by every genuine spiritual tradition. From Christian mystics, the Prayer of the Heart as spelled out by the anonymous mystic and author of *The Way of the Pilgrim*[2] is one powerful example. In another, the pilgrimage to the top of the interior mountain where the face of God is described as being shrouded in a "cloud of unknowing" is elaborated in the classic book by that name. Similarly, in the Sufi tradition, one meets the Beloved in the heart, and the dances, chants and prayers of these various Islamic sects all focus on that reality. As we've noted before, the great Indian saint, Anandamayi Ma, once instructed her listeners that: "It is only by coming to know the self that the Great Mother of All can be found." Like so many before and since she was acknowledging that the journey begins and ends right here, on the spot where you are.

And so, as we briefly consider this subject of pilgrimage, looking at the miracles of remembrance and inspiration they can afford us in the inner life, we will also keep in mind that all pilgrimages are merely external replications of the inner journey. The shrine, the temple, the sacred river is right here, right now, in you. You don't have to go anywhere to find the teertha; you are always at the crossroads. You merely have to recognize where you *are* and proceed accordingly.

After a recent pilgrimage to the ashram of the French spiritual teacher Arnaud Desjardins, in southern France, my friend Petra reported her adventures with enthusiasm. "It was so exciting to me," she said, "to again realize that spiritual practice happens only now, and that everything that comes into my life is the stuff of that practice!" She was reinforcing for herself and others that there is nowhere to go, and no waiting period in which to get your visa. You start your journey in this moment. This moment!

Tourists and Pilgrims

A recent book with the title *1000 Places To See Before You Die* was a best seller in the U.S. It immediately inspired a slew of knock-offs including *99 Places To Eat in LA Before You Die,* and *100 Books To Read* … all reflective of the desire-mad attitude of contemporary culture that, as the saying goes, "whoever dies with the most toys wins." While this *1000 Places* may be a great book for tourists, it would probably prove a complete distraction for pilgrims. The difference between a tourist in the domain of the inner life and a pilgrim is too obvious to bear making. But the question *Which one am I?* at any particular moment of my life, is always worth asking. I can be a tourist in my own home if I'm taking snapshots of happy moments as opposed to living "inside" myself and fully experiencing that happy moment. Each time I wander from the purpose I have articulated for the enrichment of my inner life, I leave the pilgrimage and climb on the tour bus, where someone else is telling me what's worth seeing or doing.

Still, the benefits of travel are extraordinary, and I'd be a fool if I didn't acknowledge that my life has been tremendously enriched by the external pilgrimages I've made. My good fortune is that essentially all of my travel has been made in the company of my spiritual teacher, so the context of pilgrimage rather than that of a vacation or tourism has always been paramount. I recall that in the early days of my apprenticeship to him we traveled over a breathtaking pass in the Alps of southern France. As I *oohed* and *aahed* at the landscape around me, he sat passively in the front seat of the car and muttered something like "seen one mountain, seen 'em all." At the time I was both shocked and annoyed by what I interpreted as his lack of appreciation for the beauty of nature, and by his consistent tendency to throw a wet blanket over my enthusiasm. Over years, however, I've come to understand that my teacher's comments were always meant for me, and had little or nothing whatever to do with the glorious scenery that surrounded us. I easily became a tourist wherever we went, and he readily caught that in my sentimental outcries. The pilgrim also might exclaim at the beauty around her, but it would be a reflection of her intention—prayer, praise, gratitude—rather than the amazement of "here *I* am in the Alps … *I'm in the Alps*, oh my God … !" Such a distinction—one self-centered, the other conscious and intentional—took me years and years to get. I'm still working that koan, truth be told, so keep that in mind as you read on.

In my teacher's company, or with his directive, I've circumambulated the sacred mountain, Arunachala, in southern India, and the ashram of his master, Yogi Ramsuratkumar in Tiruvannamalai. I've walked through Checkpoint Charlie while the Berlin Wall was still in place. I've bent down to enter the crypt of the Black Sara in the tiny church of the three Mary's at Sainte Marie de la Mer in southern France, and knelt before the altar of Our Lady of Guadalupe in Mexico City. I've visited several Zen centers and met a number of roshis, and most recently, I experienced the beauty and faith of Romanian Orthodox monasteries in the Carpathian Mountains north of Bucharest. Each of these pilgrimages, and dozens more commonplace, like the pilgrimage to my father's bedside in the tiny hospice in Rhode Island where he died, has revealed a miracle. Each has offered me a teertha through which to pass, a contact point for another world: a world in which the extraordinary has stopped or interfered, at least, with my usually predictable mind patterns, and a world in which the ordinary is suffused with the sacred. And for this, I am deeply grateful.

Around Arunachala

In 2002, on the full moon night of December, a festival known as Shivaratri, in the city of Tiruvannamalai in southern India, upwards of a million people move in swarm along the highway that circumambulates the holy mountain Arunachala. As they walk, ride in carts pulled by bicycles, or as they are wheeled in wheelchairs, or as they prostrate and rise, prostrate and rise again they chant "Arunachala Shiva, Arunachala Shiva, Arunachula Shiva" praising and invoking the blessings of the Lord of the Universe, Shiva, who in their belief is embodied in the mountain itself. The mountain is god, and god is the mountain. Simply, there is no separation.

And so, I walked this path with running shoes on, in contrast to thousands around me who made the pilgrimage barefoot, and was caught up in this human drama and this living act of prayer. Whether their purpose was to gain the god's favor for their latest engineering project, their father's glaucoma operation, or their own burning desire for liberation and enlightened insight, the song was one and the orientation to cry out to forces greater than their own human power was tangible.

Along this prayer highway the primitive and the technological were united. Whether the pilgrim came from the outlying village of untouchables, or the Brahmin had been driven in from Chennai in his Mercedes Benz, they sang the same song and the power of that song awoke the sleeping god in their own hearts and those of all the pilgrims; or at least it had this potential. One really didn't have to try to make her own intentions or guard them from the intentions of the throng. One was carried on the human wave and divine song that flooded along this well-worn highway. Individuality could be drowned in this torrent, or silenced for a few moments or a few hours, as it takes almost three and a half hours to make the entire circumambulation walking at a reasonable pace.

I have remembered this particular pilgrimage for the past three years, every month on the night of the full moon. Instead of circumambulating the sacred mountain dedicated to Lord Shiva, I pilgrimage to a tiny chapel to participate in a chanting vigil, a twenty-four-hour experience starting at midnight and extending to the following night. The chant is called Poornima, or full moon, a commemoration, and is conducted as a prayer celebrating the beloved south Indian saint, Yogi Ramsuratkumar, who lived at the foot of Mount Arunachala, and about whom I wrote an extensive biography in 2002-2003. I chant and circumambulate his statue, remembering the miracle that he was and is.

The saint was a beggar, who resided for much of his adult life on the slopes of the great mountain, and in the environs of the Shiva Temple in Tiruvannamalai. Yogi Ramsuratkumar found shelter in the caves of Arunachala, or under the awnings of shop stalls in the brass-sellers market. He was barefoot. He was unwashed. He wore rags, colorful turbans, carried a staff decorated with bits of string, feathers, scraps, and placed his treasures of old newspapers, letters, rags and assorted stuff in huge burlap bags, the kind that ragpickers carried. People thought him mad. They taunted him; threw rocks at him; startled and provoked him in attempts to drive him back to northern India from where he had come. He suffered at their hands.

Yogi Ramsuratkumar lived without a roof over his head until the 1980s when his devotees convinced him to inhabit a house they bought for him near the temple complex. Through it all he was a man of joy, a beautiful being full of light, tenderness and compassion. He danced on feet that seemed barely to touch the ground, and he sang the names of God and the *taraka* mantra, *Om Sri Ram Jai Ram Jai Jai Ram*, the mantra given him by his master, Swami Papa Ramdas. His sweet voice was high-pitched and childlike, and someone gave him the name "the Godchild of Tiruvannamalai." The slopes of Mount Arunachala knew well the touch of his calloused feet, and the rocks echoed God's name and praise as he danced and chanted along its well-worn paths.

On a cold night in December recently, as I walked around and around his statue, established in a flower-decorated shrine in the middle of the small meditation hall on my teacher's ashram in northern Arizona, I chanted his name and opened myself to melding my heart with his. On this particular night, during which I would chant from 2 until 4 AM, I was extremely restless and fighting sleep. Mind distracted, watching the clock, counting off the quarter-hours: six to go ... It occurred to me that the only thing to do would be to turn the chant over to him, as I certainly couldn't control this monkey-mind tonight. I was unable to hold focus or intention. Yet, I did trust the process that established this vigil, and opened to simply aligning myself with that. In much the way that the individual pilgrim on the road around Arunachala knows that her will is subsumed by something greater than her likes or dislikes, my job was to simply put my body on the line and allow the prayer that was echoing through me, regardless of my mind's state, to arise as unencumbered as possible.

What happened that night was invisible. With no thought or manipulation, I started to weep. The tensions of weeks of work dropped like an unnecessary raincoat. All of a sudden it occurred to me that *this* was life at the center, and that my other efforts—jobs, responsibilities, projects, wishes hopes and dreams—were out-swirlings, like the second, third or fourth layers of the mandala that unfolded from the center, the bindi point. Here, in the tiny hall, alone, in the middle of the night, I was living in purposelessness and praise, sort of how we were taught in grade school that the angels lived in heaven. There was nothing else to do, except to let myself be carried along in this mind-stopping and heart opening moment, which happily lasted and sustained for the next day. Pilgrimage is good for such purposes. One can't keep one's eyes on the finish line, nor one's intention always forefront, all the time. The pilgrim who is really lucky at some point gives up, admits that it is too hard, or too boring, or too mean-ingless, and either leaves or allows herself to get swept into a domain beyond mind and self-serving emotions, of which attraction and repulsion are primary.

The hall in which I kept this vigil was full of flowers. Stone, bronze and marble artifacts of saints and deities adorned numerous shrines. Late in the vigil, the saints and the deities honored here began to wake themselves up, in me. Instead of my devotion being directed toward wor-shiping *them*, in some way they were enlivening the very archetypal qualities they each represented, *in me.*

To a Monastery in Romania

I felt the change immediately as I sat in the airport in
Stuttgart awaiting my flight to Bucharest; a similar feeling years ago in awaiting a flight to Delhi. Before getting
on the airplane you get a sense that you are already entering a new world. These people were sturdier than the
Germans around me. And more darkly dressed. Lots of
ragtag luggage, tied with cord, being carried on board, as
they brought back the goods of the First World to their
families and friends.

Speeding through the city suburbs a few days later, en
route to monasteries in the north, we had to watch out for
wooden horse carts driven by one or two old men, hauling
firewood or trash. Gypsy women, with brilliant skirts of
day-glo orange or raspberry, supported children on their
hips or at their sides, as they walked the litter-strewn side-
walks of the villages we passed through. My companion
read to me from a small magazine devoted to news about
the scores of monasteries that nestle in the hills or along
the highways of this poignantly beautiful country. My pilgrimage had begun.

One story concerned a young monk who went to the
monastery of an esteemed elder. The young man pro-
claimed his intense desire to be transformed through the
prayer and practice that were the common lot of the initiates. Handing him a dry stick, the abbot told him to plant
it and then water it, every day, and without fail. The young
monk did as he was instructed. Despite frequent battles
with doubt and the ongoing fantasy to run away from
such a boring and apparently meaningless task, the monk
held firm in his dedication to obedience. Three years went
by before it became obvious to those around him that the

young monk's ego was drying out. As his own will shriveled, the dry twig began to show signs of life. Buds appeared, roots emerged, the stick was now a small tree and soon it flowered and ultimately bore fruit.

As we approach the convent of Varatec, in the small town of Targu Neamt, I am aware that without trying to find it, my theme or subject of contemplation for this pilgrimage has been given to me. In this "other world" that I've just entered, logic will not be the governing system. To water a twig for three years makes no sense. I understand immediately that this journey will focus on that myth known as freedom.

Varatec is home to six hundred nuns. When I tell my friends that I visited a working convent of such a number of residents they have trouble believing me. I would have questioned the fact myself if I had not been there. And Varatec is only one of many. Some nearby monasteries host two hundred monks. Another convent holds eighty. Such numbers are astounding to one raised in the anti-clerical West. The growing agnosticism of Europe, in particular, makes it difficult to comprehend that such power centers, stoked by prayer, are still in existence, and genuinely thriving.

The monastery bells sound at 5 AM, and the snow covered landscape is soon dotted with footprints made by the nuns. Some are walking briskly. Others are trudging laboriously, witness to years of arthritis or injury. I find it hard to hold back my tears as I kneel at the back of the church, at 6 AM, the official start of the day of public prayer that will continue until after 9 PM. Climbing the steps, or pulling back the heavy wooden door on the church, these women are not looking for notice or help from me or anyone else. They are on pilgrimage, they have found the teertha, and their sheer physical stamina witnesses to an intention that transcends anything less than ultimate praise of God. "*Dwam-ne-me lui-eshte*" they chant over and over in Romanian, "Lord have mercy." This word *mercy*, I find out later, is synonymous with grace: Lord, have mercy; Lord, fill me with your grace.

One by one they circumambulate the interior of the church, stopping at the various icons along the way. They begin at the back right and proceed counterclockwise through the building. At each image they linger gazing upon the face of Christ or Mary. They join their hands and then kiss the shrine. Three times they kneel and rise, each time touching their foreheads to the ground in a blazing act of humility and supplication. I am tired just watching this. I can feel the pain in my own knees after only an hour on this hard floor.

I tell this story now, as I have told it dozen of times already to interested listeners. I tell it because I want to share the impact of seeing and knowing that hundreds of my "sisters" in Romania are circling the icons of the Virgin Mary with profound devotion even while hundreds of our sisters are circumambulating the Great Mall of America in Minneapolis-St. Paul. Here, in Targu Neamt, praise and prayer lies at the foundation of women's lives. They have certainly sacrificed a great deal. But, in exchange for their renunciation, the fortunate ones have put themselves in line at the door of a vast chamber of emptiness in which the song of the universe is sung eternally. These women, and hundreds more men and women like them in this remarkable country, have chosen the inner life. They live as a brilliant and much needed counterpoint to the materialistic prison in which Western men and women have locked themselves.

I think it is important to recognize that, just like the rest of us, these women suffer doubts and conflicts, and certainly wake in the middle of a bitter cold night to ask themselves, "What am I doing this for?" It is healthy to admit that just like the "victims" of unhappy marriage who stay in the relationship because they are simply too frightened to leave, there are many men and women in religious enclosures who stay the course because they think they *should* or because they are too timid to leave. And, as evidenced from the radiant faces of so many of these nuns, there are those who are there for the sheer joy that such a life brings them. They are doing it not because they are martyrs and want to sacrifice themselves for some masochistic satisfaction; they are not praying for us because they are somehow superior to others. These people pray and live a life of voluntary simplicity, even poverty, because it is their delight to do so, even though they certainly suffer when that "delight" looks to be miles and miles far behind.

Being in Varatec I was reminded of the life of the contemporary Buddhist nun, the English woman Tenzin Palmo, who spent twelve years in a solitary cave in the Himalayas.[3] Again and again, when asked about her life and whether she expected others to follow her lead she affirmed without question that this choice was made because she loved this life. And the tenderness I saw in the faces of many of these women in Varatec demonstrated this to me.

One of my sweetest memories of the visit occurred when an elderly nun took me by the hand and guided me from an onlooker's post into the main body of the church, and sat me down in a wooden choir stall. Then, she situated herself in the stall next to mine. Choir stalls generally line the walls of Christian monastic churches. Traditionally they are meant to separate the "callers" from the "responders" in the chanting of the Divine Office, the psalms, which are sung daily. The stalls face each other across an open space, the body of the church, in which the ceremonies are often conducted. Usually a large bible or book of chants rests on a large stand in the center, and is reverently approached by the readers or choir masters.

I was the only person in the room not dressed completely in black, and I felt embarrassed and conspicuous at the thought that it would be so rude to get up and leave in a short time, even though I knew that my traveling companions were waiting for me to return from my visit so we could all go out to dinner. Despite my discomfort, however, the period in which I sat there was precious, and the impression book of my pilgrimage to Varatec contains several significant ones. The most memorable were several exchanges between the old "amma" who sat at my side and two younger nuns who approached her and venerated *her* in much the same way they had honored the icons throughout the church. Not only were these women bowing and prostrating to the gold or silver encased images of their Savior and his Blessed Mother, they were also bowing before and kissing the feet of select elders in the assembled choir. As one young nun approached, the cleanliness of her face shining in my direction, the look in her eyes as she approached this amma was that of a granddaughter approaching the grandmother who had not only taught her, but who had loved and accepted her with the unconditional regard that wise elders hold for their progeny. Love was mutually exchanged. And seeing this created an ache in me. In the next instant, as the amma placed her hand on her "daughter's" head, I cried out within my own heart for that same existential knowledge that I too was loved, no matter what!

As I came to find out later, this massive establishment (a hundred homes lying outside the monastery proper, and five or six churches, all part of it) was headed by one mother abbess, but her job was mainly administrative. The job of guidance and support in the spiritual life fell to designated ammas, elders, who each had a group in her care.

Perhaps I'd been exquisitely fortunate; perhaps I'd found the best amma in the lot and had watched the exchange with her most adoring charge. But, I don't think so. I'd like to think that what I witnessed was more the norm than the exception. And even if is was a rarity, that moment in which I was permitted to join the choir renewed in me a sense of what life might be like if our elders were honored for their wisdom, not merely because they'd lived to eighty and could still play tennis every day. The wise women I encountered here were forged, I believe, in the heat of obedience, prayer, suffering and love—the nutrients of the inner life.

At Sally's Grave

Sally's grave lies at the crest of a hill overlooking a vista that stretches for thirty miles. A barely discernible path leading to the site winds through scrub oak, sandy soil and rock. A few wooden steps lodged into the natural curve of the hillside bring the pilgrim to a small juniper tree at the base of which a small concrete block contains a statue of Hanuman, the monkey, the god, the great devotee and protector of Sita, wife of Ram. Hanuman was always one of Sally's favorites. She loved the story of the Ramayana which relates the eternal love of Sita for her beloved Ram, and the unwavering effort of Hanuman to reunite them when Sita is captured by the forces of darkness, embodied in the demon Ravana. She loved the story enough to write her own version of it—from Sita's perspective.

I climb that hill, which is close to my home, at sunset on many days and sit there by the mound of stones that marks the site where her body is laid to rest. I talk to her, not because I think she is still there, but because this place is a teertha—a doorway to another dimension; a place in which the reality of impermanence blows like a strong wind. "All things are passing," it moans, and so am I passing away, I reflect, as I look over the valley below where all my friends and family sit at their suppers. Their lives are full of this and that, without *me*! They have plans! And rightly so. Someday soon (a few years, a few decades, who knows), Regina will be only a distant memory. It is good to make a pilgrimage to a grave site and to sit here with these reminders.

On many evenings my seriousness melts into gratitude. Sally died at forty-nine years of age of cancer. She was a dynamic companion on this path of the inner life, a passionate practitioner and a deeply devoted student of her teacher. She always had an encouraging word for me and everyone. Sally was courageous. I love the fact that she didn't fall easily for the path of looking good and speaking the party line that is such a disease in any group or institution, and certainly my teacher's ashram was and is no exception.

A mother herself, Sally was dedicated to children everywhere. Without leaving the ashram, where she practiced for almost twenty years and where she died, Sally was an advocate for the health and rights of children. She wrote books that encouraged breastfeeding. She wrote stories to support the children of women in prison. She wrote about the suffering of young people whose loved ones have cancer, and so much more.

One day, five or six years after I moved to northern Arizona to be closer to my teacher and the community around him, I passed the yard where Sally was playing with some of the children. She called out to me, a smile of welcome on her face. "You don't have to be afraid to kick butt," she announced to me with her slight southern drawl and in her endearingly candid style. "You know a lot, and you can take a risk to express it," she said.

Breaking out of the box of being appropriate and good is challenging work for one raised in a religious system in which sin was so often confused with any rocking of the boat. Sally's words that day were shocking reminders that this fear of doing the wrong thing was killing my chances for escape. She was calling me to own up to the courage that she knew I had, but held back expressing. She was inviting me onto the playing field of groundlessness, where all the rulebooks were replaced by the freedom of the heart that loved others more than it cherished its own safety.

Once up on the land, making the pilgrimage to Sally's grave takes me about three to five minutes. A very short journey, but one that never fails to take me to the toll booth at the start of a very long road.

~

Werner Erhard said that it is always possible to "uplevel" your life in any moment. That "up-leveling" means that it is always possible to shift the context of your life, or to shift the viewpoint you take on any situation. We are always free to do this, Werner affirmed, making this a foundational principle of all his work.

What if my life were forever re-contexualized as pilgrimage? What if I chose, deliberately, to pare down my necessities in order to travel with fewer encumbrances? What if I chose traveling companions from among those I knew would keep me awake and alert because of their good spirit and their dedication? What if I honored my companions because they had promised to walk the path, whether they stumbled along or not, or even whether they liked the particular scenery or not? What if I went everywhere, whether to the grocery store or to the holy sepulcher of Christ, with awareness of my steps and chanting the Name of God along the way? What if I looked at everything that happened to me along any way/any Way as being a potential gift, and grace, and miracle, and instruction in the tenderizing of the heart?

Ah, what then!

Impermanence

And even if you could grasp the moment
    what would you do with it?

This sky, emblazoned with saffron.
These clouds, building fiercely on the western hills.
The images that startle, invoking awe,
the sweet sweet melodies that draw your tears,
the faces of happy children, what's to be done with them?

And should we prolong the breathing in and out
    merely to have more?
More pocketfuls of moments?
More shiny shells to be taken home and put in a jar?

And should we drink poison
enough to kill every trace of whatever
it is that lives uninvited in our flesh or bones
simply to collect more driftwood or sand dollars
to decorate a basket for a coffee table?

If only you could leap into that sky
let yourself be lightened by those clouds.
If you could only crawl into the crevasse of
a broken heart and melt there,
fired by the smiles of those children …

At last,
and with deep satisfaction,
you might have
Nothing.

                    —Regina Sara Ryan

— Chapter 8 —

Kill Your Darlings
—On Attachments—

The Tibetan Buddhist master Chögyam Trungpa
Rinpoche made a distinction that is perhaps one of the
single greatest contributions to religious scholarship and
practice of the past century. "Spiritual materialism" was his
term for the way we apply the neurosis of greed and accumulation to the domain of spirituality or the practice
of cutting through our illusions.[1] Were he alive today he
would see more and more evidence of the phenomenon,
namely, this tendency to use form, or to multiply means,
rather than to confront the end and die into the essence of
what spirit actually is.

As Trungpa so brilliantly pointed out, we grasp. *Ho
hum.* Yes, of course we do. The Buddha hit the nail on the
head with his enunciation of the second noble truth: we
grasp and therefore we suffer when we don't touch and get
to keep what we grasp for. When we can't possess all the
enticing earrings in the shop case, or when we can't afford
any of the clothes in our latest catalog, whether it is Eddie
Bauer or Victoria's Secret, it doesn't matter. It doesn't matter whether we are lusting after hiking boots and down
parkas, or bikini panties and five-inch spike heels. We suffer when we can't have them. We suffer when they arrive
in the mail and they don't fit. We suffer at the end of the

day when we don't feel happier or more fulfilled for having worn them.

And, this same strategy of grasping applies in the domain of spiritual life, as Trungpa says. The knick-knack shops and weekend enlightenment programs that advertise in the pages of yoga magazines are as distracting as the fur- and diamond-draped manikins in the shop windows along Rodeo Drive in Hollywood, or on 5th Avenue in New York City, or on the posters in the music section of the bookstore, or the Amazon.com displays promising three DVDs for the price of two.

Now, in the domain of igniting the inner life, we want not only our prayer flags, deity shrines, rosaries, candles, incense, books and weekend spa retreats, but also our bliss states, visions of Mary or Kali, sanctions of enlightenment, verifications, empowerments, nods of approval from knowing others—especially our teachers, mentors and students—but we also look to our resumes of good deeds to prove to ourselves that we really *are* okay. Welcome to the world of illusion.

Yes, this *is* our world. It is filled with enticements, and we're not going to change that. However, forewarned is forearmed. Meaning, we can practice vigilance, attention and intention to realize the extent to which we are trapped here.

Don't Grasp

The attitude or orientation of non-grasping is one of the most challenging directives I know. Personally, I want to keep the buzz … box up the glow … savor the moment by stretching it as far as possible. And yet, in my limited experience along this path I've been instructed both by my teachers and my own heart to relinquish "it," namely, everything.

One day about twenty years ago as I was taking a shower, I remembered something that I had always known but neglected. I remembered the reality of love that I've been reminding myself about in these pages. As the water poured down over my shoulders I let myself stand still, silently, letting it in, and having no words for the experience. I didn't want it to stop. But then, without conscious prompting, a choice popped into awareness. At the time I thought of it as a question being asked by God, but really that's too sticky an explanation. For lack of a better way to say it, I believed (in that moment) that I could stay in the empty bliss of this revelation, ride it, milk it, whatever, or I could surrender it to Itself (whatever that meant) and allow It to take charge and direct the next step. Remember Gibran's words about trying to direct the course of love?

Truthfully I ached a bit in choosing to move on, which I did anyway. I felt a bit like a mother might feel leaving her six-year-old in kindergarten on that first day and walking away. I loved that child, and yet to keep her at home was not what *she* seemed to want. She wanted to move forward into her life. She wanted whatever was presented next, even though on some days she loudly expressed her regret for this.

"Kill your darlings" says writer Stephen King, and he should know. He's referring to those favorite sentences, those darling supporting characters, those brilliant asides into exposition that every writer has sweated over as she's worked. Nobody wants to give them up; nobody, that is, who is not diligent in his or her primary intention. According to King, the story teller must kill any darlings that bog down or even blunt (however slightly) the sharp edge of the story being told. The forward movement of the story is all that matters. The reader needs to keep turning the pages.

The same killing of darlings applies in our circumambulation of love's mountain. Whatever is keeping us stuck at any particular rest stop, whether it is the ultra-strong cardamom flavor of the chai, or the brilliant repartee of the other travelers, or the warm glow around the heart as we look out across the meadow, or the consideration "What about *me*?" in all this ... it must be relinquished. All of it. If the love which *is* is to be kept burning at the level of intensity that we delight in, the question to ask is, "What's my aim?" or "What is my deepest delight?" or, simply "Where's the road?"

We're talking about our attachments here. We're not talking good or bad. A glass of wine, a pedicure, a Mustang, a leather purse, a house at the beach, that next breath, it doesn't matter. But, if our darlings are cushioning the shock of the story, if our darlings are distracting us from our aims, they should go. Kill them! Listen to your editor the first time she or he suggests it, or suffer the red pencil of death's demands. Whew, that sounds serious! Well, it is. Do I want to settle for a comfortable illusion, or do I want to participate in this Great Process of Divine Evolution, as my guru calls it; the Real?

You've got lots of darlings, just as I have. Some are obvious, while the darling-est are probably well disguised, like those spiritual attachments that you can't live/pray/ meditate or do yoga without. Memories are darlings too, and the nostalgia that accompanies them is a super-glue! Stuck in the "what was" we project similarly lovely scenes onto the screen of the present and the future. Because love ravaged your heart and melted all your resistance on that spring morning as you sat on the cliff overlooking the freeway into Brooklyn, or listening to the lapping waves of the Mediterranean, give 'em up. We all need to kill our darlings if we are to love *now*.

Of course, like me, you've had lots of experiences. And perhaps you fear that without being able to refer back to them you will lose a part of your identity or your motivation. "After all," the mind reasons, "those moments keep us going when the tunnel gets dark. We need them." Well, perhaps mind is right. And perhaps not. Maybe that speculation, that use of memory to stoke the fire of a past encounter is really an effort of futility. Wet and rotting leaves do not make good kindling. Dry, lifeless looking twigs, twigs with no overlay of association, no history, are the fuel that really nourishes the blaze. Be dry tinder. Be nothing. Don't reach.

Zen Teacher or Father's Daughter?

A contemporary spiritual teacher tells a story about her response to her beloved father's death. A respected teacher at the time, this woman was steeped in her tradition and highly disciplined in the ability to look upon her emotions as patterns of energy arising. When her father died, she felt strong grief. Yet, as a Zen practitioner she hesitated, momentarily wondering, *shouldn't I be less attached? Shouldn't I be more Zen-like now? Am I going to respond to Dad's death as a Zen student first and a daughter second? Or vice-versa?*

Nobly, she dropped all the labels of role, and all the "shoulds." Trusting that whatever was real in her Zen practice would inform her relationship to the event, she let herself grieve. Had she tried to act some role, she would have compromised her practice by failing to be present to the whole field, which included herself. She would have taken some past memory of some stoic icon and overlaid it on herself. It would not have fit. Everyone would have suffered, especially her.

For this teacher, as for all of us, this path is not about looking good. It is about being vibrantly alive, vibrantly feeling, thinking, emoting, working, giving, receiving … with kindness, generosity and compassion. Like us, she had to kill her darling Zen practice in order to live her genuine Zen practice. If this sounds familiar, it should. The old staying, "If you meet the Buddha on the road, kill him," communicates the same message. We can grasp at perfection and virtue with the same misguided lust we have for gold and security. Grasping, attaching, relishing our seat at the station, we miss our aim, and our train.

Don't Reach

My guru Lee uses the phrase "don't reach" when he talks about attachment and grasping. He wants us, his students, to see that many of our self-directed efforts at sadhana are misguided, since they come from ego's attempt to control the show. But, let's make an important distinction here. The opposite of "don't reach" is not "chill out, put your feet up, and have a drink." The opposite of "don't reach" is "do trust"! The difference is extreme, yet the fact is that I walk through most of my day *reaching* instead of trusting. And you?

I know that I'm reaching when I hear myself judging/ evaluating or even discussing beyond a moment's inter- est, my hair style, my body's muscular tone, my meditation practice, my boredom, my anxiety, my efficiency in travel plans, my supper menu. I waste a great deal of my "one wild and precious life" as Mary Oliver puts it, in reaching. I'll bet you do too. And yet, we can't overlay trust (like overlaying a Zen practice) on an idea. What we *can* do, as my teacher advises, is to tell the truth about *what is*— reaching is present! When I notice myself reaching, I can make a choice to drop the self-judgment associated with reaching. I can reformulate my aim. I can move on.

For me, sometimes the merest remembrance of my guru or Yogi Ramsuratkumar (my guru's guru) is enough to reorient the focus. Or the choice to shift attention from thought to physical sensation within the body does it for that precious instant. So I reach, I remember, I am reoriented. No big deal.

What you are reaching for, and the technology of your reaching style, is more or less interesting. It is good to know what possesses us so that we may be on guard when we are thrust into situations where our attachments might overwhelm our commonsense. It is useful to see that I grasp at everything, even my prison bars, which is why Lee cautions me to stop reaching. I am trapped by the myth that I am not in prison; that in fact I have some degree of freedom. In truth, unless I am actively practicing self observation, my inner life is a charade of spiritual materialism. I am a slave to my own attachments and to the attachments promoted by the media.

Radical Self Honesty

"I know myself," screams my raging neighbor, a fundamentalist Christian. *Not so*, I think. For all his generous service to his church and his years of self-examination in Alcoholics Anonymous, he remains blind to the dynamic of secrecy and righteousness that infects his relationships with his wife and his children. "I hate my Dad," says his daughter. Still, my neighbor doesn't get it. Certainly he admits to having deep remorse for the mistakes of his years of drinking, and has acknowledged that remorse to his kids and other family members. But, he remains in denial, unconscious of the ongoing nature of his relational dynamics, which are characterized by suppressed anger, shame and secrecy.

Of course my neighbor is not alone in his denial or his pain. I'm in denial too. But his case is blatant. Like so many of us, he *thinks* that he knows himself. He's taken the "12 Steps"; he's read some books; he knows the theory only too well. Trouble is, *knowing* the theory can be a huge roadblock on the path, one that can ultimately destroy any chance for an enlivened inner life.

We live in a time in which deception characterizes *everything*. We no longer trust the systems that formerly provided us with some bases of security—our churches, our government, our education institutions, and the media. Modern advertising has jaded us to the point where we accept the lies, and even spend our money to support these lies, still protesting that we know it is all hype.

I was flying to Washington state to visit a dear friend, and listening to the steward on the plane telling the passengers how pleased he was that we had chosen "his airline," and how happy he was to make our experience a pleasant one. Unfortunately, his voice sounded thoroughly flat. It must get really depressing having to represent such a promise, day in and day out, on every flight. Still, knowing it was all scripted, I found myself working hard to justify some way in which he really meant it. Then I opened the airline magazine and it was all over. I must have been in a rare mood of clarity because as I turned the pages I found nothing but lies on every one: advertisements for eye makeup that would normally have had me calculating the odds about *my* chances of ever looking like one of these models; articles about the growing tourist industry in Pittsburg, showing happy couples window shopping downtown. When I realized that I was seeing only lies yet wasn't feeling cynical, I found that interesting. Lots of people make a living out of being cynical. They're called critics. On this day I wasn't one of them. Instead, flying into Seattle with sunshine beaming everywhere, I felt sadness and tenderness, recognizing the labyrinth we were all lost in, and seeing how we were accommodating the lies for the sake of our survival. I felt great compassion, for myself and everybody else on Flight 272. So I spent the rest of the trip praying from within this tender heart.

We Are Self Satisfied

Madame Jeanne de Salzmann, a successor to G.I. Gurdjieff, in a essay comparable to a triple shot of espresso, says without apology that we are "… passive, blind and demanding." The greatest tragedy, she says, is not the blindness itself, but the denial of that blindness.

> You have no measure with which to measure yourselves. You live exclusively according to "I like" or "I don't like," you have no appreciation except for yourself. You recognize nothing above you—theoretically, logically, perhaps, but actually no. That is why you are demanding and continue to believe that everything is cheap and that you have enough in your pocket to buy everything you like.

You recognize nothing above you, either outside yourself or inside. That is why, I repeat, you have no measure and live passively according to your likes and dislikes. Yes, your "appreciation of yourself" blinds you. It is the biggest obstacle to a new life. You must be able to get over this obstacle, this threshold, before going further.[2]

Unless we are willing to admit to this type of perverse "appreciation of yourself," which I understand to mean being self satisfied, i.e., asleep, we will never work to remedy the situation. Self satisfaction creates a type of self hypnosis that keeps my comforts and my fantasies foremost, over and above everything else around me. I then find myself wandering the aisles of Victoria's Secret, enticed by a frilly pair of underpants and projecting how gorgeous they will look on my butt. But not my real butt; the smooth, tight, unblemished, airbrushed butt of my dreams.

Self-satisfied denial is having the same conversation with my husband or mother or grandson today that I had yesterday, wondering why I feel exhausted when I hang up the phone, and moving to the refrigerator for a quick snack. Blindness is turning over as I hit the snooze alarm, even though I've promised myself to get up and practice my exercises or meditate this morning. Passivity is listening to the radio or the TV, or reading the news on my I-pod phone, Twittering my life to the world, or checking my email all day long. Sleep is going away for the weekend because I'm bored or frustrated and need a break, a chance go someplace I've never been in an attempt to accomplish something. Lulled into self satisfaction I live without intention.

Who Am I Kidding?

"Who am I kidding?" is the form of self-inquiry that my guru teaches. He instructs me to use it regularly, whether I am stuck in feelings of being unappreciated, *or* when I'm feeling ecstatic, like I just got nominated for a Pulitzer. Wherever the inquiry leads, I am cautioned to keep asking the question about whatever occurs next, as I watch what happens—within the mind, the body, the emotions. Then, I ask the question again.

The results of such practice, when employed over a significant period of time, are vast and varied. For one thing, "Who am I kidding?" tends to create a new relationship to emotions. For another, it can strip away any false sense of security, exposing the lies both outside and inside. The inner life, without such a built-in form of ruthless self honesty or self observation, becomes one more fantasy excursion. Like my neighbor, one can go on for years with the mistaken belief that one *is* self-aware. Holding to this belief, life remains stalled, and sadly we don't know it. For my neighbor, it would take an even greater degree of courage and humility to extract himself from this destructive denial pattern as it did for him to admit that he was powerless over alcohol, which he did over twenty years ago.

A desire to cultivate the inner life is a call to illuminate the denials and delusions under which we (the man or woman of intent) operate. All the scriptures and traditions point to this lie we can easily buy into, this refusal to look deeply into the nature of one's own being; the refusal to tell the bottomline truth of what one sees and knows; the placement of responsibility for anything one does, or says, or thinks, outside of one's own body-mind-soul complex.

The lie can even be as subtle as an apparent prayer, like "God's will be done," if that prayer is meant as a relinquishment of what is rightly our responsibility.

"Who am I kidding?" is meant to be applied to all circumstances of our lives—the apparently nice and good things, as well as the apparently nasty bad things. We can delude ourselves with our high-minded spiritual fantasies as easily as with our dark and angry moods. We can feed the pain of separation and ego's dominance with self-congratulations as easily as with self-deprecation. And, at least in the beginning of this practice, my teacher's suggestion for using "Who am I kidding?" during the up-times has the effect of throwing a soaking wet blanket over a campfire. When times are bad, more than simply acting like the proverbial pea under the mattress, "Who am I kidding?" can be a slap in the face, a wakeup call inviting me to switch my context.

Kidding oneself is very very easy to do. Even the norm in many cases. We see it constantly in our own behavior: sleeping in when we've promised ourselves repeatedly that we would definitely get up and exercise in the morning; having that one tiny sliver of chocolate torte, or that second (or third) glass of wine, despite all our resolutions to the contrary; exploding with frustration, and perhaps even rage, when our plan is thwarted or our time schedule interrupted, by traffic, by the kids' demands, by the pokey service in the restaurant or in the checkout line in the supermarket. Such reactions get swept under the proverbial carpet all too quickly, dismissed with such justifications as, "That's just the way I am," (self-defense); "Those stupid waiters" (blame of others); "Why me, why now?" (taking things personally); "Don't those kids appreciate …" (self-pity) … the list is endless.

Who am I kidding? is meant to cut through the bullshit of self-justification, blame, self-pity, and demand a look at what's really going on. Such is the process of deepening self-knowledge. This practice builds a genuine inner life. Without a foundation of this degree of self-honesty, there is no chance of having genuine compassion for others.

Who Am I Kidding in Action

I recently went to a book conference with some colleagues and learned that my romance with wine was a much bigger distraction than I had imagined or was willing to admit. I didn't drink on this trip, but I did watch the people around me drink—some at every chance they got, and as much as they could get. I watched a friend relating to alcohol in ways that I had noticed in myself but didn't like to see: joking about it, talking about it, planning for it, desiring it and having a second one, just because she could.

There are so many things, like alcohol, that captivate our attention: food, sex, money, fancy green tea, shoes, haircuts, finger nails, jewelry, cars, tattoos. Anything and everything can become another link in the chain that keeps us from freedom. *Who am I kidding?*

A classic Zen story tells of two monks who arrived at the river and found that the bridge was washed out. A young woman stood at the water's edge, distressed at how she would get across. Although a monk is never supposed to touch a woman, the older monk simply picked her up and carried her across the stream. Hours after this event, as he walked along the road, his younger monk companion asked him how he could have done such a thing.

"Oh," said the elder. "I put the woman down as soon as we got to the other side of the river. Why are you still carrying her?"

Can I walk away from this stuff that captivates me, and walk away without residue, or will I still be carrying a desire for these things long after I've left the store, or the restaurant, or put the fancy catalog down? And what else am I kidding myself about: the need to look younger and more attractive? The need to be thought of as wise? No matter what the attachment is, these things capture my attention. They are all prison bars and I am deluded if I don't see the myth of freedom under which I labor.

"Who am I kidding?" is a mantra for our times. We are all slaves, and until we can tell the truth, we will never have the chance to be free. A story I was told at one of the Romanian monasteries I visited described a genuine monk as a "contrary" man: When he is hungry, he fasts. When he is thirsty, he often refuses to drink. When he desires something, he gives instead to others from what little he has. When he is tired, he goes to his prayers. In short, his life is dedicated to breaking those chains that the rest of humanity wears as jewelry.

How can we ever get to know who we are when we remain in prison, guarded by a moat, bars, and an electric fence of who we think we are and who we want to be. The dismantling and disassembling of this illusion is painful, and we will resist it at every step. But, what did we sign on for? To engage in the inner life is to become such a contrary.

Working in the Sanctuary

In his brilliant book *The Joy of Sacrifice*, spiritual teacher and author E.J. Gold writes: "Do not expend Power-

Center energy within the dream. Conserve it for work within the Sanctuary."[3] This quote has always inspired me. It summarizes what I've been trying to explain about the relationship between our attachments and the inner life. Mr. Gold is suggesting that the world of attachments is the dream—the world that offers us a promise of happiness, freedom from pain, and immortality. We all know that this dream is just that—a dream. Yet, daily, we keep buying our ticket for a ride on this merry-go-round, forgetting that we've already seen the futility of ever capturing that eternally-golden ring.

The point is, it takes a lot of energy to work the dream: Energy to keep up with the latest technology, for instance, lest we miss out on some amazing new way to save time and energy. Energy to cultivate those relationships that will advance our status. Energy to keep a good face. Energy to stay in shape lest we die prematurely. Energy to be a good citizen, according to some politically correct standard. This is very expensive work, and robs our inner life of the power it needs to further its deeper intentions.

What Mr. Gold means by "the Sanctuary" is worth feeling into. Notice that he capitalizes the word. The word conjures many universal applications, as you may be experiencing right now. In Judaism, for example, the Sanctuary is synonymous with the holy of holies. The simple definition of the word means the place of refuge. And don't we all need *that*? The busier our lives become, the more we are assaulted by phony promises, the more appealing the concept of sanctuary becomes.

The advertisers know this too. Which is why they are selling you new products with the word "Zen" on the label, offering you a coffee break (or now, a tea break) from the madness. They are playing on your deep desire for the true Sanctuary. But, unfortunately, their products are poisonous substitutes for the real thing. Poisonous because they insidiously placate you into believing that if only you could have this relief, this type of tea, this relaxing bath oil, all the time, you might eventually accumulate enough to approximate your heart's deepest desire. Ah well, I guess it's always been this way.

It might be worthwhile to stop here and consider for yourself what Sanctuary means, and whether or not you want it, and how much are you willing to pay for it? I don't mean pay in terms of money expended to visit a spa, but rather "pay" in the sense of attention and energy devoted to the remembrance of the Sanctuary that already exists, inside your breath. That Sanctuary may need a good dusting, or airing out, or polishing. But, don't take my word for it. Go there now and look around.

Let us tread softly here, however, since we don't want to create repercussions that we'll have to deal with later. What I mean is, let's not get too specific about the design and furnishings of this inner Sanctuary, unless directed by our guide or mentor in this practice. The Sanctuary really isn't a *place*, even if you have been instructed to, or have found, a spot within the physical body where you can "come home." This kind of physical placement is very helpful, for many of us, but I don't know that it is the exclusive path to Sanctuary. Your relationship to Sanctuary may be completely non-verbal and non-spatial. Yet, I am assuming that you do relate to the experience, with or without form, or you would probably not have engaged a book about the inner life.

What is the "work in Sanctuary" that Mr. Gold is referring to here? What is *the work* that requires power-center energy? For me, the work in Sanctuary is the work of prayer, praise, adoration and love. Praise of what? Adoration of what? Well, you tell me. I only know that praise arises, adoration arises, love arises and aligns whatever I call "me" with Itself. In that process, energy of great power is created, and I suspect that this energy is what enacts the transformation within. Love, adoration and praise also naturally overflow and influence external life—service. The work of Sanctuary, therefore, is work on behalf of others. As one individual wakes up, drops the illusions, steps into Presence, the whole field of life is affected. It has to be; it's the law. You know this is true because you've been strengthened by the witness of others, even those you've never met, simply because you *knew* they were aligned to such love. Yes? Think about the obvious ones: Mother Teresa, Nelson Mandela, the Dalai Lama. Think about the less obvious ones: your friend (actually she's my friend) in Arkansas who lives with such deliberate attention and intention.

The work in Sanctuary is the work of transformation and transmission. We are transformed and we become transmitters. That's all. If, like me, you still find yourself asking, "What about *me*?" or "What do *I* get out of this deal?" well, give yourself time. Those questions too get eaten up along with all the attachments you have to being special and important. Stay alert. Pay attention. Remember.

The Man Watching

I can tell by the way the trees beat, after
so many dull days, on my worried windowpanes,
that a storm is coming,
and I hear the far-off fields say things
I can't bear without a friend,
I can't love without a sister.

The storm, the shifter of shapes, drives on
across the woods and across time,
and the world looks as if it had no age:
the landscape, like a line in the psalm book,
is seriousness and weight and eternity.

What we choose to fight is so tiny!
What fights with us is so great!
If only we would let ourselves be dominated
as things do by some immense storm,
we would become strong too, and not need names.

When we win it's with small things,
and the triumph itself makes us small.
What is extraordinary and eternal
does not *want* to be bent by us.
I mean the Angel, who appeared
to the wrestlers of the Old Testament:
when the wrestlers' sinews
grew long like metal strings,
he felt them under his fingers
like chords of deep music.

Whoever was beaten by this Angel
(who often simply declined the fight),
went away proud and strengthened
and great from that harsh hand,
that kneaded him as if to change his shape.
Winning does not tempt that man.
That is how he grows: by being defeated, decisively,
by constantly greater beings.

—Rainer Maria Rilke, translated by Robert Bly[1]

Chapter 9

Broken, Everything

I learned recently about Naoshi—a seventeenth century Japanese style of repairing pottery using gold lacquer. A well-shaped pot, once broken, was not discarded. Even an incomplete collection of shards could be used, joined together using gold. The original jar or vase then was elevated to a wholly new level of artistic perfection. Its previously broken and now patched-together nature was transformed. Instead of being a detriment to its beauty, the brokenness was now its most distinguishing characteristic; a source of its beauty.

Poet and performance artist Leonard Cohen in his song "Anthem" reminds us that it is through the cracks in things that the light gets in. And, we know from the statements of Navajo and other Native American basket-weavers and pottery-makers that their designs are deliberately crafted with an imperfection in order that the spirit has a way in, and a way out.

We too are broken. All of us. Cracked in so many places. Flawed in the sense that an artistic creation is uneven, smudged, impermanent, flaking off. We are wounded. And so is everyone around us. One of my dear friends keeps reminding me that we too quickly forget that all "those people" with whom we have some difficulty are merely wounded. Just like us.

Our spiritual life and our prayer, then, will also be broken, since it can do no more than reflect the broken, cracked and perhaps ailing relationship we endure with life in general, with others, and with the earth. Most of us, in fact, come to spiritual practice because we have grown intensely more aware of our brokenness. We are humbled and perhaps even flattened by the circumstances around us and by the terrible news we read in the newspapers every day. We are in dire need of healing. We are in need of a potter's hand to pick up the shards of our life and meld them together again, even if it means that we may turn out a bit deformed; still, whole and therefore usable is a highly desirable state to be in.

The great teacher Thomas Merton wrote about a subject that he called "holy dread" in his book *Contemplative Prayer*.[2] He claimed that the monk, or the man or woman dedicated to contemplative prayer, needed to be enormously strong in order to bear this particular cross. Holy dread is the state of seeing ourselves fully without artifice, naked, vulnerable, mostly helpless. It is akin to what St. Paul admitted in this letter to the Romans: "I am a mortal man, sold as a slave to sin. I do not understand what I do; for I don't do what I would like to do, but instead I do what I hate." (Romans 7: 14-15). Further, in his letter to Corinth, Paul told of begging God to remove his debilitating weakness, his "thorn in his flesh." Yet he was told by God that this thorn was a gift, a constant reminding factor, without which spiritual pride might have triumphed; without which he might never learn that God's power "is greatest when you are weak."(2 Corinthians, 12: 7-10)

Is there anyone among us who cannot relate to this experience of doing the opposite of what we claim to support and intend? We are broken. And, in my view, it is important to stay on the bottom of the pile of life in order to fully feel this. Not because we want to morbidly wallow in our failures and impotencies, but because we want to be in right relationship to *what is*—namely, the brokenness of everything. Merton claims that this recognition—that an enormous and probably unbridgeable gap exists between our intuitions and intentions toward perfection (in the domain of love, service, prayer), and our thoughts, feelings and behaviors—is essential for progress in the inner life. It is exactly here, in this chasm of futility that one encounters the incalculable mercy of God. Despite our being broken, and probably because of it, the mercy of God pieces us back together with molten gold, creating of us a new vessel; humbled, glorified, and unable to forget, because we now bear in our bodies the scars of our transformation.

To look at the world from the bottom of a broken life allows us to circumvent many of the temptations to spiritual pride, one of the subtlest and perhaps deadliest forms of brokenness. Spiritual pride is deadly because it will not admit its own brokenness. Or if it will allow the admission, it will score itself points for doing so. "Oh, look how humble I am being," it will say.

A mentor of mine years ago used a phrase that I have never forgotten. Seeing my tendency to be good—a twisted survival strategy that would sacrifice being real, and the loss of relationship that comes along with that—rather than not be approved by others, by God, and especially by my illusions of myself, he looked at me one day and said, "Regina, we are either making love or making points. You can't do both at the same time."

Feeding the Broken

Another perspective on this paradox, that only we poor broken ones will inherit the kingdom of heaven, is found in the instruction on self observation given within the Fourth Way tradition. As we mentioned earlier in Chapter 2 when we discussed the foundations of the inner life, self observation is key; and only self observation without judgment is useful or effective. Judgment introduces an energy that keeps our habits in place. Lack of judgment allows some distance to develop, and with weakened identification, the habit loses momentum.

Meeting and facing the "sin" or weakness—such as our self-hatred, our dissatisfaction, our unwillingness to share, our actions that betray our belief that love is scarce—is potentially a great reminding factor, since these behaviors are so habitual. Day after day, and hundreds of times a day, if we are practicing self observation without judgment we get to look at and "eat" the energy that these habits carry. We get to wake up, if only instantaneously, using our misstep as an alarm clock. The energy is then available for inner work—for returning to the here and now; for relaxing the unnecessary tension that characterizes my stance toward life; for repeating the prayer of the heart or the name of God for the benefit of others.

It is so easy to feel and act superior when we are on the top of the heap. When something knocks us off—when we lose a loved one; when we suffer a serious setback, physically or financially; when we see a layer of meanness or fear in ourselves that we haven't seen before—we automatically understand the pain of others. We all go around pretending to be whole, trying to convince others that we've got it together. Acknowledging our fellowship with the weak and wounded we are naturally taught compassion. Hungry sinners all, we eat the substance of compassion like bread.

Another spin on life at the bottom of the heap is offered in a new book of Chögyam Trungpa Rinpoche's bearing the wonderful title, *The Mishap Lineage.*[3] The title reflects the succession of Kagyu Trungpas, an unlikely heritage of spiritual giants distinguished by their colorful lives, who made their teachings by their skillful and non-conforming dealings with the ups and downs of daily existence. In the seminar sessions transcribed in this book, Chögyam Trungpa drives home the incomparable value of being related to a lineage. At the same time, he asks us to seriously examine our tendency to want to fix mistakes—mishaps—everywhere, citing this mistaken belief as a major obstacle in our path of liberation.

As I interpret this, we are deluded in thinking that a heaven on earth is what we *should be* experiencing. Or that perfection, lack of chaos, an unhindered journey, is somehow a mark of success. The itch of incompleteness, dissatisfaction, the "never enough" and "if only" that we endure can be fuel for our practice. The insecurity that underlines everything in our world today is not the problem. The problem is the fortress we build to protect ourselves from the insecurity. "All of our lives are certainly defined by such bumps in the road, and countless small rough spots," Lee Lozowick explained recently.[4] He went on to say that "it is our practice to meet such unforeseen events directly, without freak-out, annoyance or breakdown, and move with and beyond them with grace, maturity and nobility." In other words, the question is are we facing life just *as it is* or resorting to some other-worldly paradigm to try to escape it? "Our practice … is a here-and-now Path," he said. We work with what we are given, and thus transform ourselves as we transform each and every obstacle into an opportunity for practice.

Dostoevsky on the Broken Life

There is a startling passage in *The Brothers Karamazov* in which the wise elder, the monk Fr. Zossima, speaks from his deathbed to the assembled monks. His monologue is a classic as well as a primer of the mystical life, and as such it offers refined spiritual food to those who earnestly seek it.

Zossima shockingly declares that those who enter the monastery and live the cloistered life are not *better* than those who live in the world, and in fact they are probably worse, if the truth be told. He reminds his listeners that, in all probability, they are drawn to the monastery and to the life of prayer that is fostered there *because* they would be unable to survive in any other way.

> "Love one another, Fathers," said Father Zossima, as far as Alyosha could remember afterwards. "Love God's people. Because we have come here and shut ourselves within these walls, we are no holier than those that are outside, but on the contrary, from the very fact of coming here, each of us has confessed to himself that he is worse than others, than all men on earth ... And the longer the monks lives in his seclusion, the more keenly he must recognize that. Else he would have had no reason to come here.[5]

What a refreshing perspective! All hail the monk or mystic, man or woman of prayer, alive at the very bottom of the world. Such claims turn the hierarchies of accomplishment on their heads. Genuine prayer, the mystic knows, will only come from genuine embrace of this state of brokenness.

Bringing this understanding even closer to home, the beggar saint Yogi Ramsuratkumar, whom I visited in 1995, used to refer to himself as the "dirty beggar" and the "mad sinner." And we who celebrated his awesome presence heard these claims but defended against them. "No Bhagwan," many devotees would argue, "we are the sinners and You are the saint."

I think we missed the point. I know I did. At least in the early days of my acquaintance with this radiant being, Yogi Ramsuratkumar, I could not allow myself to accept that he really meant what he said. He wasn't being humble or self-effacing as a strategy, as I might. Rather, in his awareness, being on the bottom of the social ladder was the truest place to be. He *chose* this position, not because he wanted to be special or acknowledged for it, but because it reflected the truth of what he knew about himself in relationship to the awesome mystery of what he referred to as "Father in Heaven."

Yogi Ramsuratkumar wore rags. He rarely bathed, and hence gave the appearance of being dirty. He was despicable to the righteous. He lived in squalor, or wherever he could find a roof to protect him. He was threatened, derided and even attacked by thugs and political agents, and generally dismissed by the Brahmin priesthood and sometimes even by the legitimate saffron-robed *sannyasi* of his day. One story tells of his being met by a pundit in the Shiva temple of Tiruvannamalai and walking with the man as they discussed the dharma. At one point, as they passed a *ghat*, a large pool of water within the temple complex, the pundit pushed the saint into the water, declaring, "Well now, perhaps, you will get more than one bath this year."

Despite the abuse that he received at the hands of detractors, he forgave his tormentors again and again, and refused to allow them to be punished by the authorities, even when his devotees demanded it. He lived at the bottom and therefore knew that he had no so-called rights. Or rather, that genuine rights are those granted only by God, and that these rights bear no worldly privileges whatsoever. Genuine rights were, in fact, exactly the opposite; they were a ticket to greater and more serious burdens or responsibilities that needed to be borne. The one at the bottom of the ladder is the one closest to the foundation. The one at the bottom is planted on the solid ground. The one at the bottom of the ladder is therefore responsible for keeping the ladder steady so that others may climb with confidence.

Recently, visiting my ninety-two-year-old mother, who is blind, I spent time listening to religious TV broadcasts, which are a source of great consolation and inspiration in her life. One evening a priest was giving a talk about the Holy Spirit, a subject that I tuned into with great interest. I wanted so much to be inspired by such a lofty topic. After all, the Holy Spirit is love, and the wisdom of the ages. Much to my disappointment, and even outrage at the time, what I found in the self-confidant old cleric who ran the show was a pundit, not a wise elder. His TV appearance exuded authoritativeness, and he spoke quickly the scripted sermon he'd obviously prepared with great pains.

What got to me was that he was just so damned sure of himself. So facile in answering this most profound question, "What is the Holy Spirit?" Not only was his response doctrinaire, with no life, but so dumbed down (to the point of being insulting) in order to reach the tens of thousands who were probably tuned in along with me.

Where, I asked myself, was the profound not-knowingness and awe that enables one to ascend the mountain of truth with humility, hat in hand, stunned into silence? Where was the gasp of wonder and gratitude that could precede the merest mention of the Holy Spirit? Here we were, before a mystery so great that even angels supposedly bow down before it, being offered this TV monk's perky smile and upbeat answers to his callers. My heart broke open when a man named John called in and asked, "If one is in mortal sin how can he get back the gifts of the Holy Spirit?" Here was a deeply suffering soul, a desperate soul. And what he received for his vulnerability was a platitude, a formula, and another camera-catching smile. "Okay, we have another caller on the line. God bless you John."

That night I prayed in gratitude for my association with a lineage of beggars and self-acknowledged sinners. The poet ee cummings said in his own words that as long as we are "right" we are not "young." Yes, that was it, whenever men and women are right in the sense of righteous, holy, good, they are not young. They lose their innocence, they lose beginner's mind. They lose the not knowingness that characterizes the reality of being struck down and broken open. They lose awe in the presence of mystery.

Taking Responsibility for What We Know

In the play *A Man for All Seasons*, author Robert Bolt gives words to Sir Thomas More that articulate an awesome distinction between belief and action; between simply knowing a principle and taking responsibility for it.

More was Lord Chancellor of England, a beloved friend of King Henry VIII, and a man of wisdom and great discernment. Despite More's ardent Roman Catholic faith and support of the authority of the Pope of Rome, whose directives about the validity of Henry's marriage to

Anne Boleyn were a subject of growing political implication, Sir Thomas attempted with all his skilled "lawyering" to maintain a position of neutrality. He refused to divulge his personal judgment of the case, and thus attempted to honor both the Roman Church's authority and his loyalty and friendship with his King.

But a position of neutrality within the law was not satisfactory to the King. He wanted Thomas as his advocate. Henry so much as begged his approval, which More would not give, although neither would he condemn his monarch and friend. Such neutrality was also not enough for More's detractors, those who were unconsciously threatened by such a witness of integrity. They wanted him silenced, once and for all. And so they drew up an oath of loyalty that all legislators were required to sign, a document that testified to support of the King's decision. Sir Thomas More refused to sign it, and so he was arrested, stripped of his rank and imprisoned in the Tower of London. When finally brought to trial, he argued brilliantly on his own behalf that his failure to sign the document was not an indication of disloyalty. In fact, wasn't it the law's dictum that "Silence *gives* consent" he asked. Could it not be argued, then, that his silence was actually affirming his King's right?

There was no winning in this court, however. False witnesses were brought forth, and ultimately More was accused of high treason and put to death.

At a point early in Act II, in a conversation with the Duke of Norfolk about the question of legitimate authority and the supremacy of conscience, More emphatically declares: "The Apostolic Succession of the Pope is ... Why, it's a theory, yes; you can't see it; can't touch it; it's a theory. But what matters to me is not whether it's true or not but that I believe it to be true, or rather, not that I *believe* it, but that *I* believe it … I trust I make myself obscure?"[8]

Herein lies the distinction between knowing and being. Herein arises the question, what will it take to move my "knowings about" to my integrated "being with" the principles of the inner life? To make this leap is to move from naïve adolescence to spiritual maturity. Can we say, "It is not just that I *know*, or *practice*, or *pray*," but that *I* know and practice and pray. To live in this way is to live with a sword poised above our heads at every moment. In other words, one decides to *be* a practitioner—of kindness, of obedience to legitimate spiritual authority, of active compassion, of self-observation—rather than an accumulator of knowledge, initiations, practices or the good opinions of others.

Learning the truth of this distinction is taking me a lifetime. I am forever being shown the ways in which I am broken, fail to uphold my own principles, deceive myself. And yet, I can celebrate my life, as *I* move inside rather than allow myself to be persuaded by the beliefs held by the culture of lies. My intention is aimed in the direction of self-knowledge. Dropping my self-condemnation, akin to Thomas More's shrewdness with his defamers, I can use my brokenness to fuel my sorting through a vast box of lenses. I can thus discriminate between one that promises the quick fix, myopic enlightenment, and one that allows me a long-view of genuine freedom even in the midst of my own contradictions.

Responsible for All

Dostoevsky's admonition through Father Zossima goes on:

187

... When he [the monk] realises that he is not only worse than others, but that he is responsible to all men for all and everything, for all human sins, national and individual, only then the aim of our seclusion is attained. For know, dear ones, that every one of us is undoubtedly responsible for all men and everything on earth, not merely through the general sinfulness of creation, but each one personally for all mankind and every individual man. This knowledge is the crown of life for the monk and for every man. For monks are not a special sort of men, but only what all men ought to be. Only through that knowledge, our heart grows soft with infinite, universal, inexhaustible love. Then every one of you will have the power to win over the whole world by love and to wash away the sins of the world with your tears ... Each of you keep watch over your heart and confess your sins to yourself unceasingly.[6]

The elder here reminded his listeners about what constituted the true vocation of the man or woman whose life was supposedly devoted to God. It was the true monk's destiny, Zossima affirmed, to fully take on responsibility for *all the sins of the world*; and that the entire mystical life was only valid if it brought an individual to this point of understanding: namely, "I am responsible for all."

Here is a view of the inner life both dangerous and wondrous. In other places here, and in other writings, I've noted that a life of prayer is a great contribution to others because energy can be shared, and because we are fully connected to one another; and therefore our prayers and our acts of "giving and receiving" affect, heal and support others. But this teaching is a step beyond all that. Here, Fr. Zossima asked his monks to embrace the fact that not only were they *connected* to all the sinners of the world, but they were in fact *responsible* for those sins, as well as those sinners.

It would be too easy to dismiss this teaching as being masochistic, or to walk away from it too overwhelmed with guilt or fear to be effective in addressing what it may really be pointing to. What it says is that we are not merely "connected" to all in the way that cars on a railroad train are connected, latched into each other. We are connected in the way in which organs in the human body are codependent with one another—we share the same circulatory system. The blood supply, then, must be healthy, or we're all going to suffer the consequences. If the blood supply is infected with a microorganism, some parts will manifest this infection first, and some may be affected more dynamically than others, but in the end the whole body will soon be brought down.

All the body's organs are responsible for this infection, not necessarily because they individually caused it, but because they all participate in the climate or culture of overall health that will either succumb to it or resist it. There is no good done by the liver sealing itself off from the stomach and saying, "Look, you picked up this parasite through your own gluttony; now *you* deal with it." The body doesn't work that way. The weakened consciousness of the stomach's demands is a reflection of the weakened consciousness of the whole. Every cell in the body shares in the creation of that field of consciousness, and therefore every cell is responsible.

Zossima's monks were being asked to see that they were participants in the folly that keeps humanity separate from God. By telling deeper and deeper levels of the truth about this, they are, in effect, bearing the suffering of humanity. In holding this responsibility as their own, not as some altruistic ideal of doing it for others, but with a genuine remorse of conscience for sin, they endure a transformation, a metanoia. And, because all sin is one, so is all transformation and all grace. Their transformation affects the collective soul.

Here is where I find the human witness of the life of Yogi Ramsuratkumar and other great beings to be powerful and so challenging. The beggar-saint of Tiruvannamalai was genuinely willing to take responsibility for all of it. And out of that enormous assumption of responsibility came an enormous necessity. He was responsible to pray day and night for the health of this body—an activity that we saw him engaged in continuously. When the scriptures of Christianity advise us to pray always, this is also what is being recommended. Yogi Ramsuratkumar willingly took on this job, and his example, along with the example of others like him, cannot be easily denied or dismissed.

All Sins Are Mine

We cannot place all blame for the sorry state of the world outside ourselves if we are to sincerely investigate the inner life, and live it from the bottom up. We cannot, as much as we'd like to, point to a stupid president, a greedy CEO, a gas-guzzling vehicle or a system of impersonal computer technology as being the enemy. All great religious and spiritual teachings instruct this principle: the seeds of all evil lie in every human heart. Whether I am at war with my own body or with the terrorists of some other country, I am at war! The degree of the suffering enacted is decidedly different, but the mechanism of the war-making is exactly the same.

We've heard these principles until they have become trite. *Yawn*, "Ah yes, I know. I must make peace within myself if I am to ever witness peace in the world. Pass the butter, please." And yet, it is the job of the mature spiritual practitioner to dig deeply into such ubiquitous aphorisms and resurrect the core of broken and dangerous prayer that lies within them.

One person who reportedly did this in our own time was a psychologist who worked in the prison system in the state of Hawaii.[7] Dr. Ihaleakala Hew Len's story is that he healed inmates of a hospital for the criminally insane by doing *his version* of what is known as Ho'OPonopono— an ancient Hawaiian practice of reconciliation and forgiveness. (His is not the official or only approach to this ancient methodology, but is currently the most widely disseminated.) Dr. Len apparently focused on their patient files, which reported the stories of their lives, without ever having direct counseling sessions with them. His efforts yielded powerful results. Before the institution closed, the prison went from a highly dangerous facility for inmates and staff into a peaceful place where inmates were given liberties and safely taken out of shackles.

Incarcerated men and women are generally at the very lowest rung of the social ladder. Commonly, caregivers and prison officials employ a top-dog/under-dog model in their dealings with inmates, even though we all know that ultimately this never works. The stance that these others are sick or twisted, while we (the caretakers) are blameless and whole, is a position that takes no account for the interrelatedness of all life. The very field created by such presumptions was an untenable position for Dr. Lew.

And so he determined to try a different approach. Instead of intervening behaviorally on their behalf, he took each one of their cases and in so many words "took responsibility for it." One-hundred percent! He did this by deeply working on himself, extending love and forgiveness to himself. Quite miraculously, in forgiving and releasing himself within the field of his own psychic and spiritual awareness, changes started to take place in these inmates as well. Without having to counsel them therapeutically, they began to seek for peace, for self-understanding, for reconciliation.

The roots of this practice run deep. This alternative form of healing is not foreign to many South Pacific cultures where it is used for healing both physical illness as well as rifts within families; and in the Hawaiian language this word *Ho'OPonopono* refers to putting things right, to adjusting, to amending.

Destiny Awaiting

Radical responsibility, in the way Father Zossima spoke of it, or in the way Dr. Lew practiced it, is something we may intuit as true but yet have no practice or disciple to support. Where to begin? As we've noted throughout, there is no other remedy for sleep than the willingness to admit that I am asleep. I start here. I notice my facility for placing blame outside of myself for everything that disturbs me or interferes with *my* world. I watch this habitual pattern. I watch what it does to me—inside and out. That is, I observe the high cost of such blaming and complaining and alienating and separating. I make a choice to consider something radical—namely, that I'm responsible for my view of the world. I consider forgiveness, of myself. I consider love.

As I practice—self observation, prayer, listening with the heart, forgiveness, compassion—with diligence, over time, I catch some glimpses of where my vocation and hence my broader responsibility lies. And generally, my experience verifies that one's "calling" and one's responsibility is much simpler and much more universal than the romantic destiny I fashioned for myself from my own fantasies. As I show up with more reliability in the immediate tasks that are presented to me, I am then entrusted (by God, the Universe, the Tao, my spiritual master) with more and more responsibility. This principle seems to be a natural law. It was articulated by Jesus in an enigmatic parable in which he noted that "to every person who has something, even more will be given," while "the person who has nothing, even the little that he has will be taken away from him."(Matthew 25: 14-30)

Where this willingness to listen to the offerings has led me, among other places, is into more diligent and (hopefully) more passionate writing. Surprisingly, since I have no children of my own, it has led me to organizing and implementing the childcare programs on my teacher's ashram. It has brought two young children into my immediate living situation so that I now (at age sixty-five) have two "adopted" grandchildren. As one of their caregivers and teachers, I am learning what it means to take responsibility for them—these innocent others. And I am feeling the invitation of creation to pray and witness for the needs of children throughout the world. How that will manifest, in action, remains to be shown, although the arrows are starting to shine. The circle widens, of that I have no doubt. As I come closer to the roots of myself with ever-growing self honesty, my responsibilities seem to grow in weightiness, requiring more and more refinement. At the same time, that responsibility seems to be carried more and more by the hand of That which offers it.

My guess is, therefore, that the assumption of radical responsibility is in store for anyone who seriously undertakes this journey. And I pray that we will each have the courage, strength and joy to respond to the direction in which this hand is leading us.

> If someone "Sees" for this world in one glimpse, is it not valuable for that one to sit all day "Seeing" for all, Truth, and for everyone to benefit from a "Sight" that is never lost?
>
> —Abba Jonathan of God
> hermit monk, southern Arizona desert

Mandala, native Arizona rock.

The Simple Life, No Call-Waiting

No cell phone, no caller id, no call-waiting, no
cable, no Tivo, no computer, no Ipod, no
blueberry, no notepad, no laptop, no
riding mower, no leaf blower, no weed eater,
no digital clock, no air conditioner, no new car;
I live in another country, a different century.

I ride my 3-speed bike to work, because
it helps the Earth and eases the body more gracefully
into its dying; it makes the body work hard and
it likes to work, likes to do sweat-labor despite
the avalanche of labor-saving technology whose function
is to drain us of our life force.

I write by hand in a notebook because
I like to see where I've been, follow my tracks back
through the snow to where I started, see how things
work out on the page, where I went wrong,
how to begin again, nothing deleted.
I don't want to know who's calling or

who has called. I've lived 65 years and I have
never gotten a phone call that made a difference.
If you reach me, that's fine but if you don't
nothing is lost.
Most people are slaves.
That's the way they like it.

After all the years of heartbreak and disappointment,
of treachery and betrayal, are you so far gone
that you believe the next phone call will be the one
that saves you? When Death comes for you,
you can't say, Would you mind holding?
I've got a life on the other line.

—Red Hawk[1]

196

—Chapter 10—

Practices and Prayers

Many of us are hungry for methods, ways to take us from alpha to omega in a few simple steps. Unfortunately, in my experience I've found that there are no simple steps except as one's methods are practiced with diligence, day by day, year in and year out. Few will believe this. Few will really work the method that is right under the nose. Instead, many of us would rather collect more practices, prayers and methods—and the more exotic the better, we believe—in the firm conviction that we haven't yet found *the* way in. Again, in my experience, there is no one special way in, and there is no way (special or not) that works without consistent application.

As an occasional teacher of mind training or meditation practice, I find that folks continually have questions that anticipate the problems or breakdowns that a certain practice will entail in the future. These questions arise because their minds are trying to master the method before they've actually *worked* the method. You can't learn to swim by reading a book about it, I might remind them. You can't make love with a manual in your hand.

Another drawback for many people is the "been there, tried that" attitude. They've tried to meditate, a few times, "but meditation just isn't my thing," they tell me. "My mind just goes crazy." Well, isn't that the whole point of looking in?

They've tried to practice self observation, they tell me, "But the same thought or emotion kept coming back with even greater vehemence." Reminds me of what sometimes happens when you try to call for assistance on the telephone—press #2 for a customer service representative and the original recorded announcement starts once again with all the same menu options. Help!

In each of these situations I know that a reputable teacher or experienced spiritual mentor could be of invaluable assistance. I might say that to the person inquiring. "Oh," they tell me, "I had a spiritual teacher, once, but he/she didn't help." Do we detect a pattern here? No wonder we often feel so lost, confused, even desperate! We are still looking out there for someone or something to *do* *it* to us, instead of applying focused efforts to working the programs that generations of intrepid masters and guides have given, and that our current teachers or mentors are still offering.

I can describe this situation so precisely because it reflects my own practice history. I resist the gifts. Simply put, I resist life. Still, recognizing this I can bring some degree of compassion, forgiveness, mercy to it all, thanks to the grace and guidance of my guru.

What follows here, in this last chapter, are not suggestions for new methods you should try. Rather they are descriptions of some ways in which I am currently working my program, tending the fires of my inner life. If these suggestions offer you inspiration to return to the core teachings of your original faith tradition, or inspire you to seek out genuine help in the person of a spiritual counselor, or guru or lama, or simply remind you of long-neglected prayers and practices that you've given up on for any number of reasons—excuses?—well, my delight and responsibility is to offer something here that may be more than straw in a turbulent sea.

1. The Blessing Walk

In some of my seminars I urge the participants to take a blessing walk in the middle of the afternoon. I instruct them to simply extend blessings in all directions with whatever they encounter along the way. When they return from this simple exercise they usually report some very dramatic re-orientations. Their view has shifted, and for that they are enormously grateful.

For me, to bless is not the sole prerogative of the saint or designated holy person, although is the common understanding of the term. To bless is not the sole prerogative of God, either, I think. Even the dictionary would seem to concur with me, as it offers "to make holy by religious rite; sanctify" as its first definition, and "to invoke divine favor upon" as its third option. In either case, one could argue that we are all capable of blessing one another insofar as we are willing to make all things holy by our ways of viewing them; and we can all invoke divine favor on a person, place or thing, by our conscious consent to the Divine Mystery alive in us, and in which we live.

"Bless" derives from the old Germanic *bloedsian* which meant to consecrate or sprinkle with blood, as occurred during sacrificial rituals. Here again, the extension of the meaning might be useful to us. To consecrate means to "make sacred"—you can do that—and "with blood" could just as easily refer to your *prana* or life force, or that substance that fuels your genuine heart of compassion.

To confine blessing as the privilege of God's hands *alone* may be an expression of profound faith, even of surrender. It might also be an unconscious cop-out, expressing our unwillingness to *be* God's hands, i.e., to do God's Work, on earth. We might all do well to contemplate this question.

Nonetheless, to wish one another good fortune, to shine compassionate eyes on one another, to cease our separative judgments and instead take on the practice of prayer as we walk through our lives seems to me like a worthy occupation. It's all about the view we wish to cultivate. We can begin to see things differently, and we can also begin to see ourselves differently if we recognize that we have the ability and perhaps even the obligation to bless everything.

What if has been a question we've asked at several junctures in this book. So let's address it again here. *What if* you took a walk and "blessed" whatever you encountered along the way, with conscious intention? *What if* you sat at a café or in a waiting room and "blessed" or "consecrated" whomever entered or whomever came to mind? *What if* you greeted or said good-bye to loved ones with "Blessings" or "I bless you"? *What if* you deliberately asked others to please bless you, and reminded them that you were blessing them at the same time? *What if* you knew without question that your blessing was a dynamic invocation, a true prayer, a compassionate ripple in the matrix of energy field that holds our world together?

2. Cremation Practice

The Indian cremation ground is called a *smashan*. There, both the tourist and the serious practitioner can sit and contemplate the reality of impermanence, that everything changes and that we are all going to die. Here the witness gets to observe with fewer buffers than usual the raw fact that he or she is on a pilgrimage to this same place.

For some remarkable Indian sects, like the aghoris, meditation in the smashan is integral to their "remembering" of their purpose for living.[2] It provides them with a doorway to the heart of the Divine Beloved, who is accessible insofar as the grasping for self satisfaction and the attachment to anything less than Absolute Love has been annihilated in the cremation fires. For the serious aghori, as diligently instructed and guarded by his or her guru, the fires of everyday life may become a traveling cremation ground. Such a one can transform every activity, by intention and self-remembering, into prayer and practice and praise of that Reality.

Without any illusions that I have a fraction of the discipline and passion for God that the aghori represents, I know that my own life offers me continual opportunities for a pre-school variety of cremation ground practice. I also know that I miss even these opportunities unless I'm on the lookout for them. Let's take long distance travel as one simple example. I travel to Europe, sometimes once or twice a year, for seminars or book conventions. At my height, six-foot-three, the airline seats in economy class are, to put it nicely, significantly cramped. Conversations with fellow passengers, before, during or after the flight, generally deteriorate into shared complaint sessions as we support one another in the conviction that we *will be*, *are*, or *were* suffering unjustly for our eight or more hours aboard.

So, here I am on an airplane, with a handy cremation ground in which to practice contemplation of impermanence, and in which to feed my longing for the Beloved, and what do I do with this precious gift? Generally I waste it.

How easy it is for me to fantasize about some exotic trip to Benares, there to sit on the banks of the Ganges and watch the bodies consumed by fire. There to see without doubt that my life is short and growing shorter by the minute; there to recreate my intention to love and serve, as soon as I get home. Meanwhile, the potential grace of a currently uncomfortable situation (like this long distance flight) gets co-opted by thoughts and feelings of outrage and self-pity. I am trapped in the survival instinct, convinced at some level that I *have* to move or I will die! No wonder I'm so exhausted at the end of the trip; I've been actively resisting the simple *what is* of my life for the last twelve hours.

A story I heard recently drove home this point about resistance for me. The revered French spiritual master Arnaud Desjardins travels frequently from France to Canada, where he has an active body of students. When he arrived in Quebec on a recent trip, one of his Canadian hosts remarked that, while many in his traveling party looked bedraggled from the long hours of travel, Arnaud looked relaxed and ready to get to work. The master smiled and replied with one word, "Nonduality." Simple. Monsieur Desjardins was not caught in the usual fight of resistance that most of us engage as our modus operandi. His reference to nonduality instructed his students that he was "one with" whatever was presented to him.

My own practice of late has become an investigation into this constant resistance to the *what is*—the constant "No" that characterizes my life activities and relationships. Without judging myself negatively for this, or without even trying to change the thought or behavior, I am attempting to observe these NOS. I routinely try to leave the cremation ground, to separate myself from raw reality— from you, or from anything else that threatens my illusion of survival. I've taken to saying "always separating" to myself when I notice this.

I also frequently say NO to watching documentaries about the world's poor and suffering. I easily say NO to physical labor that puts me outside my comfort zone, like gardening in the Arizona sun even when our community garden is in sore need of upkeep. I try to say NO to spending a long period of time with an annoying sangha mate or co-worker. I say NO to missing sleep. I resist the weather, the temperature in the car, the discomforts of any kind of travel. I internally fight with products on the shelves in grocery stores, because I judge them too sugary, or too highly processed, or whatever. I resist the newsstand fashion magazines because I have separated the realm of high fashion from the realm of what is supposedly spiritual. I still say NO to dirty, smelly or even to poorly dressed people, even if in my heart *I wish I could* accept them. I even say NO to staying too close to my teacher, who is a living smashan fire. He's okay in small doses, but the truth that he will burn me—reducing my illusions to ash—is only too obvious. And for that I'm also enormously grateful.

I think it is vital to tell the truth about our NO before we can stumble into YES. I think that our lives are rich with opportunities to pilgrimage to the river banks of Mother Ganga—the Goddess of Life and Death—there to be instructed in the nature of impermanence and the precious nature of human life. Such observations immediately become opportunities to remember a new possibility for internal relaxation, for prayer, for re-contexualizing the moment's experience. Consciously *choosing* to stay present and attentive in the current smashan, in whatever form that cremation ground shows up, transforms my life now, and now, and now.

3. Using Sacred Artifacts

At a Buddhist center not far from my home I heard a story that continues to inspire me. A woman who was attending a program there asked the teacher, Venerable Garchen Rinpoche, for help. She told him that she was dying, and had been given a short time to live. What should she do during this time? The master instructed her to recognize first of all that her body was merely a guest house, and that she should anticipate leaving the guest house as it was no longer useful for her. But secondly, he advised her in the meantime to "contemplate sacred images." It didn't matter whether the image was of Christ or Buddha or Mary or some saint or another deity. The point was to realize that this sacred image represented *her truest nature*. Here was a simple practice that could make her remaining months or years useful to herself, and ultimately to others.

I especially liked this story because my teacher trades in sacred artifacts. He runs several art galleries in which these sacred images from numerous spiritual traditions can be experienced, and purchased. He encourages me and others to surround ourselves with sacred images, to use them to create sanctuary for ourselves in our homes and even in our offices and places of business, as appropriate.

We live in a time in which the sacred is being trivialized by its application to herbal teas and room deodorizers. We live in a time in which our TVs and computers become our household shrines. We live in a time in which collecting more and more stuff has become a real burden, requiring more and more precious life energy to maintain. We have always lived in times in which the remembering of our essential nature has been a great challenge.

The use of sacred artifacts could be one valuable means to counter the constant forgetfulness of aim and purpose. The use of sacred artifacts could be a way to transform our homes into places of deep abiding rest; to create a mood that ignites the longing for God, truth, reality. The use of sacred artifacts could be a way to communicate a faith dimension to our children without needing to preach about anything. Sacred artifacts can serve to focus our attention and lead us into prayer and contemplation.

My husband Jere and I love the image of Our Lady of Guadalupe, the Divine Mother who appeared in Mexico City centuries ago. We live in the U.S. Southwest, so we find her image in Mexican restaurants, on T-shirts worn by tough looking teens, on plastic jewelry and even emblazoned on lunch boxes. At a certain point I get uncomfortable with this, as it seems like more marketing hype. On the other hand, when I can recognize my tendency for always separating, I can use these opportunities for prayer and blessing, rather than as something to complain about.

Great art, created with high intention—like some of the world's great cathedrals or *stupas* or mosques—is more than a mere reminding factor. Great art is actually a doorway into a type of psycho-physical reorientation. We enter into such places and we are literally changed! This is why such places become sites of pilgrimage. Add to this the fact that millions of ardent prayers expressed in one place build an energy within that space—an energy that can be tapped, used, shared.

The inner life may be suffering because we are not supporting it in our outer life. Surrounding ourselves with art and sacred images can become a way to encourage remembrance of what is essential, and the truest intentions of our longing hearts.

4. Unplugging

This subject merits an entire book, I think. But the word alone, contemplated seriously, is a good start. The inner life is destroyed in small increments, not in big explosions. It is destroyed by the insidious whittling away of our vital life force through the tiny choices that comprise our days. Our worldview has been changed by technology, certainly, and not always for the better. If we become slaves to our technology we must recognize that something is off.

The poem by Red Hawk that opens this chapter makes this point better than I ever could. It takes serious courage to stand in the face of the lie of "more better faster." But then again, how seriously are we committed to igniting the inner life?

5. Cultivating Good Company: Conversations of the Heart

To keep good company is a most beneficial way of igniting the inner life. Certainly we are all inspired by certain men and women whose lives intersect with ours, but how often have we made the effort to sit with them, to share a cup of tea, to simply call them on the phone? A pilgrimage to meet with those you would consider good company in your vicinity may be as simple as visiting the nursing home where Gloria is confined to bed with MS, or having lunch with Aunt Joan who spends her time helping the elderly get to their doctors or other appointments on time. For those with some connection to a church or spiritual group, the possibilities for good company are strong. For those without such connections, keeping good company becomes an even greater necessity.

The distinction between just "getting together" and cultivating the conversations of the heart is vital here, however. Even among groups of deeply committed individuals, the conversations may stay superficial, never venturing to the domain where the heart may be opened, touched, inspired, or in which a real issue may be wrestled with. Sometimes it takes a bit of skill to get this sort of ball rolling, as filler conversations are the norm.

I have spent lots of time with really great people simply talking about our shared history, comparing notes on where we've been, what teachers we've studied with, where we've gone on retreat—all what Chögyam Trungpa Rinpoche would call "spiritual materialism." I leave these exchanges tired and uninspired. Curiosity is not a strong enough foundation on which to build relationship. Even with my close sisters and brothers on the path, our dates together are more often about a cup of coffee or a movie and a meal rather than a means to explore the vast landscape of our mutual love and commitment. There is nothing wrong with celebrating whatever forms our communion takes. Nonetheless, there are always new horizons to explore. Horizons that may reveal new discoveries, about ourselves and one another.

Who knows how to ask questions that unlock our aims and aspirations and longings? When Joanne returned recently from a two-week solitary retreat I asked her "What did you get on retreat that would be useful for me to hear?" My question hit the mark. It opened a conversation of the heart about prayer, always a favorite subject. How much more enlivening that conversation was than some generic overview of her experience.

Some of the people who've most inspired my life have been people whose hunger for truth, for something real, has overflowed into their no-nonsense approach to conversation. I call my friend Elizabeth only a few times a year, but our exchanges never fail to enrich me. We share a common love for prayer and for devotion to Mother Mary. I call her to reignite these fires.

Point is, we generally waste a huge amount of energy in useless talking. It takes courage to break this cycle. The breaking of the cycle only happens by making ourselves aware of how we use our speech, so we're back again to self observation.

Well now, this question of how we waste energy by useless or draining conversation would be one among many interesting topics to explore with someone you respect. If you do experiment in this domain of good company and conversations of the heart please consider writing me a note to tell me about your explorations. I think the subject bears lots more investigation. I am on the Way with you—please inspire me!

Endnotes

Introduction

1. *The Cloud of Unknowing and Other Works*, translated by Clifton Wolters, New York: Viking Penguin, reprinted 1978, 68.

Chapter 1

1. "How long have we forgotten how to listen!" translated by Ruth and Matthew Mead from THE SEEKER AND OTHER POEMS by Nelly Sachs, translated by Ruth and Matthew Mead and Michael Hamburger. Translation copyright © 1970 by Farrar, Straus & Giroux, Inc. Reprinted by permission of Farrar, Straus and Giroux, LLC.
2. Eve Ensler, *Insecure At Last, A Political Memoir*, New York: Villard, 2008, xx.

Chapter 2

1. Antonio Machado, "Last Night as I was Sleeping" from *Times Alone: Selected Poem of Antonio Machado,* © 1983, by Antonio Machado and reprinted by permission of Wesleyan University Press.
2. Chögyam Trungpa Rinpoche, *Great Eastern Sun, The Wisdom of Shambhala*, Boston, Massachusetts: Shambhala Publishers, 2000, 34.

3. "We awaken in Christ's body" by Symeon the New
Theologian from THE ENLIGHTENED HEART: AN
ANTHOLOGY OF SACRED POETRY, EDITED by
STEPHEN MITCHELL. Copyright © 1989 by Stephen
Mitchell. Reprinted by permission of HarperCollins Publishers.
4. "On Love" from THE PROPHET by Kahlil Gibran,
copyright 1923 by Kahlil Gibran and renewed 1951 by
Administrators C.T.A. of Kahlil Gibran Estate and Mary G.
Gibran. Used by permission of Alfred A. Knopf, a division of
Random House, Inc.
5. Baul song quoted in: Kshitimohan Sen, *Medieval
Mysticism of India,* New Delhi: Oriental Book Reprint
Corporation, 1974, 202.

Chapter 3

1. Red Hawk, *Wreckage With a Beating Heart,* Prescott,
Arizona: Hohm Press, 2005, 154, used with permission.
2. Mr. Lee Khêpâ Baul [Lee Lozowick], *The Eccentricities,
Idiosyncrasies, and Sacred Utterances Of A Contemporary
Western Baul,* Prescott, Arizona: Hohm Press, 1991, 27-28.
3. Lalitha, personal communication, April 2010.
4. "Keeping quiet" from EXTRAVAGARIA by Pablo
Neruda, translated by Alastair Reid. Translation copyright
© 1974 by Alastair Reid. Reprinted by permission of Farrar,
Straus and Giroux, LLC.

Chapter 4

1. *New and Selected Poems: Volume One* by Mary Oliver.
Copyright © 1992 by Mary Oliver. Reprinted by permission
of Beacon Press, Boston.

2. Lee Lozowick, *The Little Book of Lies and Other Myths*, Prescott, Arizona: Hohm Press, 2005, 223-226.
3. Regina Sara Ryan, *Praying Dangerously: Radical Reliance on God*, Prescott, Arizona: Hohm Press, 2001, xi-xii.
4. www.grandmotherscouncil.com

Chapter 5

1. These two poems of Hafez are previously unpublished renditions, © Vraje Abramian, March 2010. Translated from the Farsi from original source: *The Complete Divan of Hafez of Shiraz* / edited by Dr. Hosein Pejman Bakhtiari.Tehran, Iran: Forooqhi Publications, 1984.
2. Sheikh Abol-Hasan of Kharaqan, renditions by Vraje Abramian, *The Soul and a Loaf of Bread*. Prescott, Arizona: Hohm Press, 2010, 32.
3. "On Love" from THE PROPHET by Kahlil Gibran, copyright 1923 by Kahlil Gibran and renewed 1951 by Administrators C.T.A. of Kahlil Gibran Estate and Mary G. Gibran. Used by permission of Alfred A. Knopf, a division of Random House, Inc.
4. Wendell Berry, "Poetry and Marriage: The Use of Old Forms (1982)," in Wendell Berry, *Standing by Words*, North Point Press, 1983, 205.
5. Carlos Castenada, *The Wheel of Time, The Shamans of Ancient Mexico, Their Thoughts about Life, Death and the Universe*. Los Angeles: LA Eidolona Press, 1998, 19.
6. See: http://cancer.ucsd.edu/outreach/PublicEducation/ CAMs/arttherapy.asp Additional resources at: The American Association for Art Therapy, 1202 Allanson Road, Mundelein, IL, 60060-3808; (888) 290-0878; www.arttherapy.org Arts and Healing Network, PMB 612, 3450 Sacramento Street, San Francisco, CA 94118; Fax: (415) 771-3696; www.artheals.org

Chapter 6

1. Rumi, *Say I Am You: Poetry Interspersed with Stories of Rumi and Shams,* Translated by John Moyne and Coleman Barks, used with permission, Maypop, 1994.
2. Jane Kenyon, "Happiness" from Collected *Poems.* Copyright © 1996 by The Estate of Jane Kenyon. Reprinted with the permission of Graywolf Press, Minneapolis, Minnesota, www.graywolfpress.org.
3. Dr. Reggie Ray, *Elephant Magazine,* "busyness is laziness," Autumn, 2005, 20-21.
4. From a compilation of stories by Ma Devaki, *Saranagatham,* Publication of the Yogi Ramsuratkumar Trust, Tiruvannamalai, India, March 2004, 39.
5. Excerpt from "A Ritual to Read to Each Other" taken from *A Scripture of Leaves,* by William Stafford, © 1989, 1999 William Stafford/The Estate of William Stafford. Published by Brethren Press. www.brethrenpress.com. Reprinted with permission.
6. See*: Mother Teresa: Come Be My Light,* edited and with commentary by Brian Kolodiejchuk, M.C. New York: Doubleday, 2007.
7. Kathleen Norris, *Acedia & me: A Marriage, Monks, and A Writer's Life,* New York: Riverhead Books, 2008.
8. Kathryn Hulme, *Undiscovered Country: The Search for Gurdjieff.* Revised edition. Lexington, Kentucky, Natural Bridge Editions, 1997, 81.
9. Richard Schiffman, *Mother of All: A revelation of the Motherhood of God in the life and teachings of Jillellamudi Mother,* San Diego: Blue Dove Press, 2001, 312
10. Joan Sutherland, "This Floating World," *Shambhala Sun Magazine,* March 2005, 73.
11. Lee Lozowick, *Gasping for Air in a Vacuum: Poems and Prayers to Yogi Ramsuratkumar,* Prescott, Arizona: Hohm Press, 2004, 722

12. Katherine Mansfield, "Bliss," in *The Best Short Stories of the Modern Age*, selected by Douglas Angus, New York: Fawcett Premier, 1974, 91.

Chapter 7

1. Pesha Gertler was Seattle's Poet Populist for 2005-2006. Her second chapbook, titled, *The Healing Time: Finally on my way to Yes* is now available for $10 plus $2 postage to: Pesha Joyce Gertler, P.O. Box 75464, Seattle, WA 98175-0464. This poem is used with her kind personal permission.
2. *The Way of a Pilgrim*, translated by Olga Savin, Boston: Shambhala, 1991.
3. Vicki Mackenzie, *Cave in the Snow Tenzin Palmo's Quest for Enlightenment*, Bloomsbury USA, 1999.

Chapter 8

1. See: Chögyam Trungpa Rinpoche, *Cutting Through Spiritual Materialism*, Boston: Shambhala, 1987.
2. Jeanne de Salzmann, "The First Initiation" was originally published in *Gurdjieff: Essays and Reflections on the Man and His Teaching*, New York: Continuum, 1996, edited by Jacob Needleman and George Baker, from the French edition compiled by Bruno de Panafieu.
3. E. J. Gold, *The Joy of Sacrifice*, Nevada City, California: IDHHB and Hohm Press, 1978, 130-131.

Chapter 9

1. "The Man Watching" from SELECTED POEMS OF RAINER MARIA RILKE, A TRANSLATION FROM THE GERMAN AND COMMENTARY by ROBERT

BLY. Copyright © 1981 by Robert Bly. Reprinted by permission of HarperCollins Publishers.

2. Thomas Merton, *Contemplative Prayer*. New York: Image Books, Doubleday, 1969.

3. Chögyam Trungpa Rinpoche, *The Mishap Lineage: Transforming Confusion Into Wisdom*, Boston: Shambhala, 2009.

4. Lee Lozowick, December 13, 2009, Darshan address. Unpublished.

5. Fyodor Dostoevsky, *The Brothers Karamazov*, translated by Constance Garnett; New York: Barnes and Noble Classics, 2004, 155.

6. Op. cit, 155-56.

7. http://www.idreamcatcher.com/hooponopono/ It should be noted that this approach by Dr. Lew is not the exclusive definition of this practice. Readers are advised to do their own further investigation.

8. Robert Bolt, *A Man for All Seasons*, New York: Scholastic Book Services, 1960, 53.

Chapter 10

1. Red Hawk, *Self Observation, The Awakening of Conscience, An Owner's Manual*. Prescott, Arizona: Hohm Press, 2009, 110. Used with permission.

2. See the work of Robert E. Svoboda, particularly: *Aghora: At the Left Hand of God*: Brotherhood of Life: Albuquerque, New Mexico: 1986.

Select Bibliography

Bernbaum, Edwin. *The Way to Shambhala, A Search for the Mythical Kingdom Beyond the Himalayas*, New York: Doubleday Anchor, 1980.

The Cloud of Unknowing and Other Works, trans. by Clifton Wolters, New York: Viking Penguin, reprinted 1978.

Gold, E. J. *The Joy of Sacrifice,* Nevada City, California: IDHHB and Hohm Press, 1978.

Kingsley, Peter, *In the Dark Places of Wisdom*; Inverness, California: The Golden Sufi Center, 1999.

Lozowick, Lee. *Feast or Famine: Teachings on Mind and Emotions.* Prescott, Arizona: Hohm Press, 2008.

Mackenzie , Vicki, *Cave in the Snow: Tenzin Palmo's Quest for Enlightenment*, Bloomsbury USA, 1999.

Merton, Thomas, *Contemplative Prayer.* New York: Image Books, Doubleday, 1969.

Norris, Kathleen, *Acedia & me: A Marriage, Monks, and A Writer's Life*, New York: Riverhead Books, 2008.

Red Hawk, *Self-Observation: the awakening of conscience.* Prescott, Arizona: Hohm Press, 2009.

Red Hawk. *Wreckage With a Beating Heart—Poems,* Prescott, Arizona: Hohm Press, 2005.

Ryan, Regina Sara, *Praying Dangerously: Radical Reliance on God,* Prescott, Arizona: Hohm Press, 2001.

Schiffman, Richard, *Mother of All: A revelation of the Motherhood of God in the life and teachings of Jillellamudi Mother,* San Diego: Blue Dove Press, 2001.

Trungpa, Chögyam Rinpoche. *Cutting Through Spiritual Materialism,* Boston: Shambhala Publications, 2008.

Trungpa, Chögyam Rinpoche. *Great Eastern Sun: The Wisdom of Shambhala,* Boston: Shambhala Publications, 2001.

The Way of a Pilgrim. Trans. by Olga Savin, Boston: Shambhala, 1991.

Index

of self, 33
and self observation, 180
without, 39, 45
justification, 170-171
Justin Parvu, Father, 5-9

K

Kali, Goddess, 4, 113
Kagyu Trungpas, 181
kali yuga, 4, 7, 53-54
keeping the edge, 26, 27
"Keeping Quiet" [Neruda], 48-49
Kenyon, Jane ["Happiness"], 91-92
"kill your darlings" [King], 161-162
Kingsley, Peter, quoted ix-x
Kolam, 51-52
"Know Thyself," 10, 37-39, 46
Krishna, *see* Radha and

L

Lalitha, quoted, 46
"Last night as I was sleeping" [Machado], 12
Len, Dr. Ihaleakala Hew, 191-192
life force, *see* prana
light, relationship to, 137
lineage, 181
listening, inner, 44
love
    as cosmic law, 80
    in Dostoevsky novel, 182

and Dr. Goodheart, 70-74
as ground of all, 68-69, 83
madness of, 78
also see devotion
Lozowick, Lee
    his activities, 113-114
    author's experience with, 95, 103, 143-144
    book [*Feast or Famine*], 38
    on facing life just as it is, 181
    as living prayer, 63-64
    and memorizing scriptures, 8-9
    his poems / prayers to Yogi Ramsuratkumar, v, 123-124
    quoted, xiii, 43, 54, 95, 111
    on not reaching, 164-165
    on relaxation, 125
    and saying something useful, xv-xvi

M

Machado, Antonio, 12
macrocosm / microcosm, 20, 23
Magnificat, 25
Man for All Seasons, A [Bolt], 185-187
"Man Watching, The" [Rilke], 176
mandala, 33, 51-53, 148
maner manush, (man of the heart), 30
Mansfield, Katherine [*Bliss*], 135
mantra, 53, 55, 147
Mary, Mother of Jesus, 24-27, 208

Maureen, author's friend, 9
"me in God," *see* "God in me"
mechanicality / mechanical life, 3, 46, 124
meditation, practice of, 47-49, 67, 197
mentor, *see* guru; witness
mercy, 59, 151, 179, 198
merit, accumulation of, 120
Merton, Thomas [*Contemplative Prayer*], 178, 179
methods, 197-198
microcosm, *see* macrocosm
mind
    dominance of, 106-107
    surrendering of, 147-148
    watching the, 49
    also see self observation
More, Sir Thomas, 185-187
Mother Teresa, 104-105
Muktananda, Swami, 138
Mystical Body of Christ, 96

N

name of God, 53-55
Naoshi, 177
Neruda, Pablo ["Keeping Quiet"], 48-49
No, to life, 202
nobility, *see* intrinsic dignity
nonduality, 202
non-separation, 23, 83; *also see* love; separation
noonday devil, 108-109
Norris, Kathleen, 101, 108-109
"no top end" [Lozowick], 95
"not good enough," 36

O

obsessing, 69
Oliver, Mary [*The Summer Day*], 50
"organic innocence" [Lozowick], xiii

P

Palmo, Tenzin, 152
Parmenides, x
perpetual motion, 89-97
pilgrimage, 141-157
    around Arunachala, 145-148
    as context, xii, 157
    to cremation ground, 201-203
    life as a, 70, 83
    of movie actress, 115
    to Romania, ix, 149-154
    to Sally's grave, 154-156
    and vigil, 147-148
Ponticus, Evagrius [*The Praktikos*], 108-109
pottery, 177
practice, spiritual, 121, 193
prana, 26
prayer, 51-64
    brokenness and, 182
    definitions of, 55, 61-63
    distinctions about, 19, 60-61
    of the guru, 63-64
    interior, 55
    immature, 57
    mature, 60-61
    for others, 60
    of petition, 56-59

in Romanian convent, 149-151
silence and, 105
waking up the deity, 55
also see mantra; name of God;
work in Sanctuary
Prayer of the Heart, 142
Praying Dangerously [Ryan],
xi, 56
present moment, 39
presence, *see* being-presence
Pythagoras, x

R

Radha and Krishna, worship
of, 28
Ramayana, 154
Rangoli, 51
rasa(s) of devotion, 78
Ray, Dr. Reggie, quoted, 93
reaching, 164-165; *also see*
grasping
Red Hawk, poetry by, 32, 196,
206
book by, 37-38
relax / relaxation, 121-122, 124,
125, 131, 133
"religion of one" [Norris], 101
resist / resistance, 198, 202
responsibility / responsible,
187-190, 192-194
retreat, author's experiences on,
120-121
Rilke, Rainer Maria ["The Man
Watching"], 176
risks / risk-taking, 113, 114
Roberts, Bernadette, 23
Rodin Museum, 84

Romania, *see* pilgrimage, to
Romania
Romanian Orthodox
Christians, 5
Romans, letter to, 178
Ross, Elisabeth Kübler, 16
Rumi, 102, 114-115, ["The
Guest House"], 88

S

Sachs, Nelly, xviii
sacred artifacts / images, *see*
artifacts
sacrifice, *see* tapas
Sally's grave, 154
Salzmann, Jeanne de, 167-168
sanctuary, 172-175
San Diego Medical Center, 86
Saint Francis of Assisi, 28
Saint John the Baptist, 78-79
Saint Paul, 178
Saint Symeon, 22-23, 29
scriptures, 8
self-denial, 116, 118
self honesty, 165-167
self inquiry, 169-172
self loathing, 18
self observation, 19, 33-49; 169-
172; 180
Self Observation [Red Hawk],
37-38
self pity, 170-171
self satisfied, 167-168
sentimentality / sentimentalismo, 16, 57, 134-139
separation, 3, 27, 125, 170; *also
see* non-separation

223

work in Sanctuary, 174, 175;
also see sanctuary
wounded, 128, 177-178
"wise innocence" [Lozowick],
see organic innocence

Y

Yes, to life, 45, 128, 130, 203
Yogi Ramsuratkumar
author's book about, 122,
132-133
asking Lee to speak, xv-xvi
Lee's reference to, 29; *also see*
Lozowick

and life on Arunachala, 146-147
as "mad sinner and dirty
beggar," 183-184
quoted, 60
like the sun, 94
taking on responsibility for
all, 190

Z

Zen monks, 172
Zen teacher, 163-164
Zossima, Father, 182, 187-188,
192

Mandala, colored sand.

Other Titles of Interest from Hohm Press

PRAYING DANGEROUSLY
Radical Reliance on God

by Regina Sara Ryan

Praying Dangerously re-enlivens an age-old tradition of prayer as an expression of radical reliance on God, or non-compromising surrender to Life *as it is. This approach* expands the possibilities of prayer, elevating it beyond ordinary pleas for help, comfort, security and prosperity. *Praying Dangerously* invites a renewal of the inner life, by increasing one's desire to burn away superficial, safe notions of God, holiness, satisfaction and peace.

Paper, 240 pages, $14.95   ISBN: 978-1-8990772-06-2

THE WOMAN AWAKE
Feminine Wisdom for Spiritual Life

by Regina Sara Ryan

Through the stories and insights of great women whom the author has met or been guided by in her own journey, this book highlights many faces of the Divine Feminine: the silence, the solitude, the service, the power, the compassion, the art, the darkness, the sexuality. Read about: the Sufi poetess Rabia (8th century) and contemporary Sufi master Irina Tweedie; Hildegard of Bingen, author Kathryn Hulme (*The Nun's Story;* German.healer and mystic Dina Rees, and others. Includes personal interviews with contemplative Christian monk Mother Tessa Bielecki; artist Meinrad Craighead and Zen teacher and anthropologist Joan Halifax.

Paper; 20+ photos; 518 pages; $19.95   ISBN: 978-0-934252-79-9

ONLY GOD
A Biography of Yogi Ramsuratkumar

by Regina Sara Ryan

This powerful biography introduces the life and teaching work of the contemporary beggar-saint Yogi Ramsuratkumar (1918-2001) who lived on the streets of Tiruvannamalai, India. "Only God" was his creed, and his approach to everyday life. It reflected his absolute faith in the one transcendent and all-pervasive unity which he affectionately called "My Father." The biography is an inspiring mix of storytelling, interviews and fact-finding.

Hardback, 30+ photos, 832 pages, $39.95   ISBN: 978-1-890772-35-2

AS IT IS
A Year on the Road with a Tantric Teacher

by M. Young

A first-hand account of a one-year journey around the world in the company of *tantric* teacher Lee Lozowick. This book catalogues the trials and wonders of day-to-day interactions between a teacher and his students, and presents a broad range of his teachings given in seminars from San Francisco, California to Rishikesh, India. *As It Is* considers the core principles of *tantra*, including non-duality, compassion (the Bodhisattva ideal), service to others, and transformation within daily life. Written as a narrative, this captivating book will appeal to practitioners of *any* spiritual path. Readers interested in a life of clarity, genuine creativity, wisdom and harmony will find this an invaluable resource.

Paper, 848 pages, 24 b&w photos, $29.95   ISBN: 978-0-934252-99-7

FEAST OR FAMINE
Teaching on Mind and Emotions

by Lee Lozowick

This book focuses on core issues related to human suffering: the mind that doesn't "Know Thyself," and the emotions that create terrifying imbalance and unhappiness. The author, a spiritual teacher for over 35 years, details the working of mind and emotions, offering practical interventions for when they are raging out of control. A practical handbook for meditators and anyone dedicated to "work on self." Lee Lozowick has written over twenty books, including: *Conscious Parenting; The Alchemy of Transformation;* and *The Alchemy of Love and Sex*; and has been translated and published in French, German, Spanish, Portuguese and other languages.

Paper, 256 pages, $19.95   ISBN: 978-1-890772-79-6

SELF OBSERVATION ~ THE AWAKENING OF CONSCIENCE
An Owner's Manual

by Red Hawk

This book is an in-depth examination of the much needed process of "self" study known as self observation. It offers the most direct, non-pharmaceutical means of healing the attention dysfunction which plagues contemporary culture. Self observation, the author asserts, is the most ancient, scientific, and proven means to develop conscience, this crucial inner guide to awakening and a moral life.

This book is for the lay-reader, both the beginner and the advanced student of self observation. No other book on the market examines this practice in such detail.

Paper, 160 pages, $14.95   ISBN: 978-1-890772-92-5

WREAKAGE WITH A BEATING HEART

poems by RedHawk

Red Hawk's poetry has long been acclaimed by his fellow poets, Pulitzer Prize winners and National Book Award Finalists, for its gutsy honesty, plain language, and consummate skill. Never is that poetic skill in rendering the truth more evident than in this, his fifth book of poetry. This collection contains a series of sonnets, some of which he has been working on for thirty years.

Paper, 300 pages, $16.95   ISBN: 978-1-890772-50-5

NOBODY SON OF NOBODY
Poems of Shaikh Abu-Saeed Abhil-Kheir

Renditions by Vraje Abramian

Anyone who has found a resonance with the love-intoxicated poetry of Rumi will profit from the poetry of Shaikh Abil-Kheir. This renowned but little known Sufi mystic of the 10th century preceded Rumi by over two hundred years on the same path of annihilation into God. This book contains translations and poetic renderings of 195 short selections from the original Farsi, the language in which Abil-Kheir wrote.

These poems deal with the longing for union with God, the desire to know the Real from the false, the inexpressible beauty of creation when seen through the eyes of Love, and the many attitudes of heart, mind and feeling that are necessary to those who would find the Beloved, The Friend, in this life.

Paper, 104 pages, $12.95   ISBN: 978-1-890772-08-6

HALFWAY UP THE MOUNTAIN
The Error of Premature Claims to Enlightenment

by Mariana Caplan

Dozens of first-hand interviews with students, respected spiritual teachers and masters, together with broad research are synthesized here to assist readers in avoiding the pitfalls of the spiritual path. Topics include: mistaking mystical experience for enlightenment; ego inflation, power and corruption among spiritual leaders; the question of the need for a teacher; disillusionment on the path … and much more.

Paper, 600 pages, ~~$21.95~~ $11.00 available as Publisher's Seconds only
ISBN: 978-0-934252-91-1

WOMEN CALLED TO THE PATH OF RUMI
The Way of the Whirling Dervish

by Shakina Reinhertz

This book shares the experience of Turning practice by women of the Mevlevi Order of Whirling Dervishes. The beauty and mystery of the Whirling Dervishes have captured the mythic imagination of the Western world for centuries. Rumi, the great Sufi saint of 13th-century Turkey, taught both male and female students this whirling dance, but in the centuries after his death women were excluded from participation. Not until the late 1970s, when Shaikh Suleyman Dede brought the turn ritual to America, was this practice again opened to women. The heart of the book is the personal experience of contemporary women—interviews with over two dozen American initiates (from adolescents to wise elders), many of whom have practiced on this path for twenty years or more.

Paper, 300 pages; 200 B & W photos and illustrations; $23.95
ISBN: 978-1-890772-04-8

JOURNEY TO HEAVENLY MOUNTAIN
An American's Pilgrimage to the Heart of Buddhism in Modern China

by Jay Martin

"I came to China to live in Buddhist monasteries and to revisit my soul," writes best-selling American author and distinguished scholar Jay Martin of his 1998 pilgrimage. This book is an account of one man's spiritual journey. His intention? To penetrate the soul of China and its wisdom. Anyone who has wondered about the health of monastic Buddhism in China today will find this a fascinating revelation. Anyone who longs for the serenity and clarity that the author sought will want to read this book.

"Well written and intelligent." – *Library Journal*

Paper; 263 pages; b&w photographs, $16.95
ISBN: 978-1-890772-17-8

YOU HAVE THE RIGHT TO REMAIN SILENT
Bringing Meditation to Life

by Rick Lewis

With sparkling clarity and humor, Rick Lewis explains exactly what meditation can offer to those who are ready to establish an island of sanity in the midst of an active life. This book is a comprehensive look at everything a beginner would need to start a meditation practice, including how to befriend an overactive mind and how to bring the fruits of meditation into all aspects of daily life. Experienced meditators will also find refreshing perspectives to both nourish and refine their practice.

Paper, 201 pages, $14.95   ISBN: 978-1-890772-23-9

THE ANTI-WISDOM MANUAL
Ways and Means to Fail on the Spiritual Path

by Gilles Farcet, Ph.D.

What if the spiritual path turned out to be a road to hell paved with good intentions? Most spiritual books tell us what we *should* do, or how we *should* view things. *The Anti-Wisdom Manual* takes a different approach. It simply describes what people *actually do* to sabotage their own progress on the spiritual path, whatever their chosen way – Christian, Buddhist, Native American, Muslim, Jewish, or any other. Think of it as a handbook in reverse. Using humor and irony, while based in clarity and compassion, the author alerts readers to the common traps into which so many sincere seekers easily fall.

Paper, 176 pages, $14.95   ISBN: 978-1-890772-42-0

ZEN TRASH
The Irreverent and Sacred Teaching Stories of Lee Lozowick

Edited and with Commentary by Sylvan Incao

This book contains dozens of teaching stories from many world religious traditions—including Zen, Christianity, Tibetan Buddhism, Sufism and Hinduism—rendered with a twist of humor, irony or provocation by contemporary spiritual teacher Lee Lozowick. They are compiled from thirty years of Lozowick's talks and seminars in the U.S., Canada, Europe, Mexico and India.

These stories will typically confound the mind and challenge any conventional seriousness about the spiritual path. In essence, however, they hold what every traditional teaching story has always held—the possibility of glimpsing reality, beyond the multiple illusions that surround the truth. Lozowick's unique style makes these stories contemporary and practical.

Paper, 150 pages, $12.95   ISBN: 978-1-890772-21-5

MARROW OF FLAME
Poems of the Spiritual Journey

by Dorothy Walters   Foreword by Andrew Harvey

This compilation of 105 new poems documents and celebrates the author's interior journey of *kundalini* awakening. Her poems cut through the boundaries of religious provincialism to the essence of longing, love and union that supports every authentic spiritual tradition, as she writes of the Mother Goddess, as well as of Krishna, Rumi, Bodhidharma, Hildegard of Bingen, and many others. Best-selling spiritual author and poet Andrew Harvey has written the book's Introduction. His commentary illuminates aspects of Dorothy's spiritual life and highlights the "unfailing craft" of her poems.

Paper, 144 pages, $12.00   ISBN: 978-0-934252-96-6

STAINLESS HEART
The Wisdom of Remorse

by Clelia Vahni

Anyone who has ever felt guilt will find both comfort and direction in this clearly written and compassionate book. The "stainless heart" is Clelia Vahni's description of the pure, essential nature of the human being. This heart, however, is rarely touched. One reason for this impasse, the author states, is that we have built walls around the heart out of shame, or have held ourselves apart so we don't get hurt or hurt others any more because we are afraid of the pain that guilt carries. Guilt is different from genuine remorse, the author argues. Guilt destroys us, while true remorse is the entry into truth, to a clear vision of life "as it is," and thus to a transformed relationship to ourselves and others.

Paper, 160 pages, $12.95   ISBN: 978-1-890772-40-6

NO CHILD IN MY LIFE*

by Regina Sara Ryan

A practical resource for men or women grieving over the loss of a relationship with a child. The author recognizes that grief can be equally painful for people who have lost children in custody settlements, or through illness or accident, or given children for adoption, or never had a child due to infertility, miscarriage, abortion, or for other reasons of chance or choice. Offers step-by-step guidance through the stories of those who have used their pain to grow into a deeper connection to truth, life, or God.

Paper, 256 pages, $12.95   ISBN: 978-0-913299-93-7
*Originally published by Stillpoint, this book is now available through Hohm Press

AFTER SURGERY, ILLNESS, OR TRAUMA**
10 Practical Steps to Renewed Energy and Health

by Regina Sara Ryan,   Foreword by John W. Travis, M.D.

This book fills the important need of helping us survive and even thrive through our necessary "down-time" in recuperating from surgery, trauma, or illness. Whether you are recovering at home or in the hospital for a few days, weeks, or even months, this book will be your guide to a more balanced and even productive recovery. It follows a wellness approach that addresses: managing and reducing pain; coping with fear, anger, frustration and other unexpected emotions; inspiration for renewed life, becoming an active participant in your own healing; dealing with well-meaning visitors and caregivers…and more.

Paper, 285 pages, $14.95   ISBN: 978-0-934252-95-9
**This book is now a publication of KALINDI PRESS, an affiliate of Hohm Press

Poetry Credits

page xviii
"How long have we forgotten how to listen!" translated by Ruth and Matthew Mead from THE SEEKER AND OTHER POEMS by Nelly Sachs, translated by Ruth and Matthew Mead and Michael Hamburger. Translation copyright © 1970 by Farrar, Straus & Giroux, Inc. Reprinted by permission of Farrar, Straus and Giroux, LLC.

page 12
Antonio Machado, "Last Night as I was Sleeping" from *Times Alone: Selected Poem of Antonio Machado,* © 1983, by Antonio Machado and reprinted by permission of Wesleyan University Press.

pages 22–23
"We awaken in Christ's body" by Symeon the New Theologian from THE ENLIGHTENED HEART: AN ANTHOLOGY OF SACRED POETRY, EDITED by STEPHEN MITCHELL. Copyright © 1989 by Stephen Mitchell. Reprinted by permission of HarperCollins Publishers.

pages 23, 69
"On Love" from THE PROPHET by Kahlil Gibran, copyright 1923 by Kahlil Gibran and renewed 1951 by Administrators C.T.A. of Kahlil Gibran Estate and Mary G. Gibran. Used by permission of Alfred A. Knopf, a division of Random House, Inc.

pages 32, 196
Red Hawk, *Wreckage With a Beating Heart,* Prescott, Arizona: Hohm Press, 2005, 154, used with permission of the publisher and author.

pages 48–49
"Keeping quiet" from EXTRAVAGARIA by Pablo Neruda, translated by Alastair Reid. Translation copyright © 1974 by Alastair Reid. Reprinted by permission of Farrar, Straus and Giroux, LLC.

About the Author

Regina Sara Ryan has studied contemplation and mysticism for over forty years. Leaving a Catholic convent where she lived and worked as a nun during the 1960s, she began to explore many religious traditions, particularly inspired by the lives of the great women of Hinduism, Christianity, Buddhism and Sufism. Since meeting her own spiritual mentor, the Western Baul master Lee Lozowick in 1984, Regina has continued to follow what she calls a path of "unashamed devotion" in which she works to bring her life of contemplation into action. She has written in the field of spiritual life, including *The Woman Awake* and *Praying Dangerously*, as well as in holistic health and wellness, *The Wellness Workbook* (coauthored with John W. Travis, M.D.). Regina conducts seminars and retreats in the U.S. and Europe. She lives with her husband in Paulden, Arizona.

Contact: c/o Hohm Press, PO Box 31, Prescott, Arizona, USA; 928-778-9189; hppublisher@cableone.net

About Hohm Press

Hohm Press is committed to publishing books that provide readers with alternatives to the materialistic values of the current culture, and promote self-awareness, the recognition of interdependence, and compassion. Our subject areas include parenting, religious studies, women's studies, the arts and poetry.

Contact Information: Hohm Press, PO Box 31, Prescott, Arizona, USA; 928-778-9189 • hppublisher@cableone.net

Visit us on the web at: www.hohmpress.com